An Exposure to Sports

A Reflection of My Involvement in Sports as a Participant, Spectator, and Coach

by

William G. "Billy" Coward

Billy Coward

DORRANCE PUBLISHING CO., INC.
PITTSBURGH, PENNSYLVANIA 15222

Dorrance Publishing Co., Inc.
701 Smithfield Street
Pittsburgh, PA 15222
Visit our website at *www.dorrancebookstore.com*

ISBN: 978-1-4349-2929-7
eISBN: 978-1-4349-2281-6

This book is dedicated to
my father, the late John E. "Jerry" Coward;
my grandfather, the late Dr. W. George Avant;
and my great-uncle, the late Dr. Frank W. Avant,
who were all athletes and sports enthusiasts.
Each of them paved the way for me and my interest in sports.

Preface

My life has been influenced in different ways by many of the individuals whom I have met along the way as a result of my involvement in sports: several teachers and coaches who have served, unknowingly, as role models or mentors; many of my teammates from junior high school to college and beyond, who have challenged me and given me the courage to reach beyond my perceived ability; and the many young people with mental and physical challenges whom I have met who did not let their impairments prevent them from achieving their goals.

A young man, who was on a semi-pro basketball team that I coached years ago, had lost an arm as a result of an accident when he was a child. But he learned to use his disadvantage to his advantage as a basketball and baseball player. His accomplishments were phenomenal – he played far better in both sports than many two-armed individuals did in either sport. A young lady whom I met years ago had polio at a very young age but ended up playing basketball and running track and became a gold-medal winner in the Olympics. As a water-safety instructor, I have worked with young children with mental or physical challenges and others with hearing impairments and speech impediments who participated in the International Deaf Olympics, which I was privileged to participate in as an official at the University of Maryland years ago, but who managed to achieve their goals in spite of many obstacles. Each of these individuals has inspired me beyond belief, and I fervently believe I am a better person for having met them.

My involvement in sports has also given me the opportunity to meet many individuals who are distinguished for their accomplishments in one sport or another as well as the opportunity to play with or coach individuals who later became well-known. These individuals and the circumstances under which I met them are mentioned in this book.

This book is a chronicle of my lifelong involvement in sports – the contributions I have made to the various sports and the benefits I have received as a result of my involvement in football, basketball, baseball, track, tennis, and swimming; and more importantly, the individuals whom I have met along the way, many of whom have become lifelong friends who have enriched my life.

I am very fortunate to have been able to live a long and productive life and for this I am truly thankful.

Table of Contents

Chapter 1

FOR AS LONG as I can remember, I have had a fascination with and an interest in sports – particularly football, basketball, baseball, swimming, track, and tennis. My interest in sports was probably influenced by my father, John E. Coward, who was also a sports enthusiast, first as a player and later in his life as a promoter. "Jerry," as he was known to most, attended Durham State Normal School in Durham, North Carolina, in the early 1920s, where he played baseball and football. Several of his former teammates and classmates have told me the story about a baseball game between Durham State Normal School and Howard University on an Easter Monday in Durham in 1924, in which my father played. As the story goes, the game was tied 2-2 in the last of the ninth inning. Runners were on first and third bases when my father came up to the plate as the next batter. I was told that in those days there were gamblers who frequented the games, and one of them came out onto the field and put some money – about twenty dollars – on home plate and said to my father, "Buddash," (my father's nickname), "bring the run in and that money is yours." Dad put down a bunt down the third-base line, picked up the money off home plate, and headed for first base. The runner from third base came in and scored, and my father was so fast that he was safe at first base. The game was over and Durham State Normal had won. Each time this story was told, there was a lot of laughing and backslapping.

In 1925 the name of Durham State Normal School was changed to North Carolina College for Negroes and more recently to North Carolina Central University. My father, as a member of the football team, and other students had the opportunity to vote on the school colors and mascot for the newly-named school, chose the colors maroon and gray and also selected the eagle as the school's mascot. He played quarterback on the first football team for North Carolina College for Negroes.

Other family members who influenced my desire to participate in sports were my maternal grandfather, Dr. W. George Avant, and his brother, Dr. Frank W. Avant. As students, they attended Howard University and were on the University's first football team in 1893. Uncle Frank was captain of the first team at Howard and, after graduating, coached at Shaw University in Raleigh, North Carolina, and Lincoln University in Pennsylvania.

During the 1893 football season, funds had not been allocated for uniforms or equipment for the Howard University team. Consequently, the team's uniforms consisted of whatever old clothing or used equipment the team could scrounge up. My grandfather somehow learned that a teacher on campus, Miss Ella Smith, was a friend of William Lewis, an outstanding center on Harvard University's football team. My grandfather asked Miss Smith if she would write a letter to Mr. Lewis asking for his assistance in obtaining any castoff uniforms the Harvard team might have. The response wasn't immediate, but she persisted and, after a short period of time, they received enough uniforms from Harvard to equip Howard's entire team.

As a native-born Washingtonian, I grew up in the Northwest section of town; more specifically, in the LeDroit Park section at 2nd and W streets during the late 1930s and early 1940s. I was exposed to and participated in sports at a very early age. Although we didn't have many facilities for sports, we improvised and played many of our games in the street. We played one- and two-hand touch football, and occasionally, we would have to stop the game when a car came by and wait for the car to pass before continuing the game. We also played kickball in the streets and used the four corners of an intersection as the bases. We would kick a rubber ball and run around the bases designated as first base, second base, third base, and home plate. More than once, the police came by to stop us from playing in the street.

When we played touch football on a larger scale, we moved our game to Gage Elementary School at 2nd and V streets. Otherwise, we would have had to walk quite a distance to another playground. We had to climb the fence to get onto the Gage playground. We weren't permitted to use the playground because Gage Elementary School was for white children. The 1930s were long before integration in the schools began. We could only play touch football there because the surface was too rough. If we wanted to play tackle football, there was a pipe yard with a grassy area located on 2nd Street between W and Bryant streets. I think that pipe yard is still there after more than seventy years. On Saturday mornings the fellows in the neighborhood got together and went to Howard University below the library to an area suitable for tackle football. We had many outstanding tackle football games there. We played there until a security guard approached and told us to leave. But we continued to go back again and again on Saturdays, knowing we would be asked to leave at some point. When we played touch football at Gage, I would play with my older brother, Jerry Leon, whom our family called Leon and who was three years and nine months older than I. The other fellows were also older and larger than I was. But they would choose me on their team because I could catch the ball and hold on to it for a fellow my age and size. Frequently players on the opposing team would leave me alone, thinking that I wasn't a threat, but on those occasions, I became the receiving player for a touchdown pass.

When we played softball in the Gage schoolyard, it was a very exciting time because the players could hit the ball over the fence for a home run. Unfortunately, there were homes on the other side of the fence on Flagler Street and more than once someone broke a window. I can only imagine how irate those homeowners must have been, but I don't recall that anyone in our group was ever reprimanded for any of the broken windows.

We also lived about three blocks away from the old Griffith Stadium on 5th Street, right behind the Howard University medical and dental schools. The Howard University Hospital now occupies that site. Fans attending the baseball or football games at Griffith Stadium routinely parked their cars in the neighborhood because there wasn't a very large parking lot on the premises of Griffith Stadium. During the baseball season, we could hear cheering from the crowds when the home team scored or made a terrific play. I recall when the Redskins were playing there, you could hear the roar of the crowd, and Harry Wismer, the radio broadcaster at that time, would bellow with excitement when the Redskins scored.

In the late 1930s, a young teenager by the name of Abe Pollin lived just a couple of blocks from where I lived on 1st Street near W Street, Northwest. He later became famous by purchasing the Baltimore Bullets basketball team and then bringing the team to Largo, Maryland, in Prince Georges County, where they played for a number of years before moving to the District of Columbia. After the move to DC, the team's name was changed to the Washington Wizards. Mr. Pollin was also responsible for building the Capitol Center in Largo and then the Comcast Center (since renamed the Verizon

Center) in downtown Washington between 6th and 7th streets and F and G streets. The Washington Wizards and the Washington Capitols hockey team currently play their home games at this facility. The construction of the Verizon Center was instrumental in the revitalization of downtown Washington.

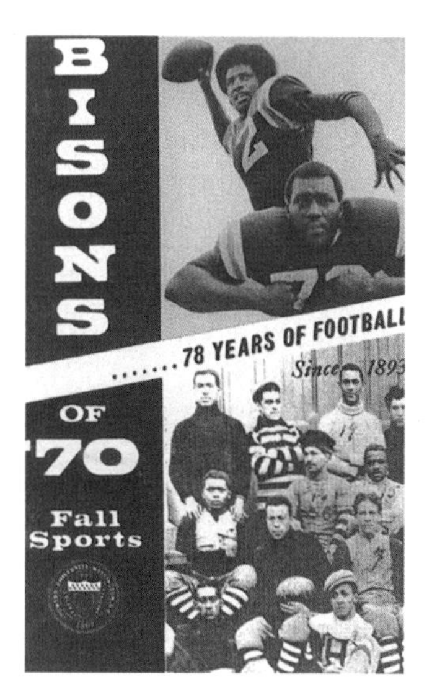

Courtesy Howard University Sports Information Dept.
Howard University Football 1970 Media Guide

Courtesy Moorland Spingarn Research Center, Howard University
Howard University's first football team 1893
Sitting in first row: Billy Coward's uncle, Dr. Frank W. Avant,
Howard's first football team captain
Standing in the third row: Billy Coward's grandfather, Dr. W. George Avant

B. Coward's Personal Collection
Durham State Normal Baseball Team, State Champions in 1924, now North Carolina Central University.
Billy Coward's father, John E. "Jerry" Coward, is located fourth from the right.

B. Coward's Personal Collection
Billy Coward's father, John E. "Jerry" Coward, in 1924.

B. Coward's Personal Collection
Billy Coward's brother, Jerry Leon Coward, & friend Charlie Malone.

B. Coward's Personal Collection
First Row left to right: Booker T. Brooks, my brother Jerry Leon Coward, Billy Coward,
Arthur Elms, Rennsaler Shorter.
Second Row left to right: Tony Christian, Billy Prather, George Bryant.

Chapter 2

BECAUSE OF THEIR mutual interest in sports, my father along with Eric "Ric" Roberts, a former football player with Clark College in Atlanta, Georgia, and a sportswriter for the *Pittsburgh Courier* newspaper, and Charles "C.C." Coley, a very close college friend of my father's, gave origin to and became the three original promoters of the Capital Classic Football Game in 1942. The concept of the Capital Classic was to get two of the best teams from historically black colleges or powerhouse teams during that era to participate in an annual "classic" game. Some of the participating college teams were Morgan State, Kentucky State, Virginia State, West Virginia State, North Carolina College, North Carolina A&T, Florida A&M, Tennessee State, and Tuskegee's Army-Air Force. The games were played at night at the old Griffith Stadium.

People from up and down the East Coast frequented the games. There was a great deal of camaraderie, friendship, fun, and enjoyment among those in attendance. There was a Battle of the Bands during the extravagant half-time ceremonies. I remember fondly how Tuskegee's Army-Air Force (TAAF) band performed at halftime during one of the Classic games. All of the stadium lights were turned off, and the TAAF band appeared on the field with small flashlights mounted on their shoes. As they marched in synchronization, the audience saw only the pattern made by the lights as the band played a very catchy marching song. The crowd whistled and applauded loudly.

Entertainers, such as Louis Jordan and Cab Calloway, performed during the halftime as a part of the pageantry that included the crowning of Miss Capital Classic and the queens from the two participating colleges. And, of course, there was always a fireworks display at the end of the halftime performances. I recall being the ball boy at several of the games. The promoters wanted the game football as well as the Classic to be unique, so they purchased white leather footballs as well as yellow leather footballs, each with two black stripes around them. The drawback was that the balls blended in with the colors of the teams' jerseys if they were wearing white or yellow and it was hard to know who was carrying or who had the ball. Because of this, all games played after 1948 were played with the conventional brown balls with two white stripes around them.

More than 168,000 fans attended the games in eight years. (See the "Original Famous Capital Classic" collage of pictures at the end of this chapter which includes scores and the number in attendance for each game.)

Harold Jackson, a graduate of Dunbar High School in DC and Howard University, was hired to be the public-address announcer for the Capital Classic games. He was also the P.A. announcer for the Washington Lichtman Bears basketball team, the Washington Homestead Gray's baseball team, and the sports announcer for radio station WINX at various times during his career. I was unaware of it at the time, but Mr. Jackson was to have a great influence on my exposure to sports.

In 1943, I enrolled in Garnet Patterson Junior High School. I played on the school's touch football, basketball, softball, and track teams. Before school integration, the schools in the Division II system in the city were Banneker, Brown, Francis, Garnet Patterson, Randall, and Shaw junior high schools. In those days, we were separated into two groups: the lightweight teams and the heavyweight teams. The lightweight teams were comprised of athletes weighing 112 pounds or less. Players on the heavyweight teams weighed 113 pounds or more. I played on the lightweight teams. In my ninth-grade year, we won the city basketball championship for the Division II school system, and I was fortunate enough to be awarded the Walker Memorial medal, awarded to the outstanding athlete in the school.

My brother, Leon, preceded me in attending Garnet Patterson and later at Dunbar High School. While attending Dunbar, Leon lettered in football and was the manager of the track team. Upon graduation from Dunbar, he received a football scholarship to North Carolina College (now North Carolina Central University). I have not given my brother credit for his influence on my decision to play sports, but he was a role model for me.

I recall an incident that happened to me many years ago as a young teenager that has been imbedded in my memory. In 1945 my family moved to the 3600 block of 11th Street, Northwest. We were the first "colored" family in the block. One of the neighbors who befriended me was an Italian-American about my age whose name was Tony. Tony lived directly behind me on 13th Street. We often played catch with our baseball and gloves in the alley behind our homes. One day Tony invited me to go to Raymond playground behind Raymond Elementary School at 10th Street and Spring Road, a short walk from our homes. He wanted me to meet some of his friends and play baseball with them. I asked my mother, and she gave me permission to go. The next day after school, we went to the playground, and Tony introduced me to several of his friends. Among them were a young Pat Buchanan and Warner Wolf. Buchanan later became a presidential candidate and a political analyst. Warner became a sports announcer on Channel 9 in Washington and later with a station in New York. We had gone to the playground on several occasions without incident. But one day as we were playing, two police officers approached me. One of them told me I could not play there. I asked, "Why not?" and explained to him that I lived only a block and a half from the playground. He told me I had to go down to Banneker playground to play and if I didn't leave or if I came back, he would have to arrest me. Banneker is about twenty blocks away from the Raymond playground. I surmised someone had called the police when they saw me playing with the other teenagers, who were all white.

As a result of not having access to playgrounds in the neighborhood because of segregation, we improvised by putting peach baskets on telephone poles in the alleys in back of our homes. In some instances where individuals had garages behind their homes, they would go to a sporting goods store and purchase a basketball set, which included a basketball, basketball rim, strings, and backboard, to erect as high as possible on the garage and hopefully no lower than ten feet from the ground. We played one-on-one, two-on-two, or three-on-three in the limited space we had. I recall a lot of fun-filled rough and physical games with many of my friends in those days.

During the 1945-1946 basketball season, Harold Jackson, the public-address announcer for the Lichtman Bears basketball team, took over the operation of the Bears team. They then became known as the Washington Bears. Harold Jackson was kind enough to give me passes to see their games. The Bears' home games were played at the old Turner's Arena located at 14th and W streets, Northwest. The games were played on Sunday afternoons. As a warm-up to the Bears' games, local teams from the various sections of Washington played preliminary games. Some of the names of the players on the Bears' roster were "Pop" Gates, "Tee" Carver, Jackie Bethards, Jerry Cooper, "Red" Briscoe, "Dolly" King, Johnny Isaacs, Bill "Rookie" Brown, "Sugar" Cain, Zach Clayton, and player-coach "Tarzan" Cooper. Not all of these players were local; several of them traveled to DC from their hometowns for the games. Johnny Isaacs, Pop Gates, and Dolly King lived in New York; Rookie Brown, Zach Clayton, and Tarzan Cooper lived in Philadelphia, and Sugar Cain came from Baltimore. Many of these players were known only by their nicknames. Sam Lacy, the sportswriter for the Afro-American newspaper, used to referee some of the Bears basketball games at Turner's Arena.

Bill "Rookie" Brown was very popular at the time because he made a movie and played the leading role in *The Harlem Globetrotters*. Zach Clayton later became better known when he was the boxing referee in the ring for the World Heavyweight Championship fight between Mohammed Ali and George Foreman. Sugar Cain was a physical education teacher and basketball coach at Dunbar High school in Baltimore, Maryland.

Arnold "Red" Auerbach, who had graduated from George Washington University, was in the Navy during that time, and stationed in Norfolk, Virginia. He contacted the Bears organization to schedule a game with a team of players from the Navy, including himself. Other players on that team were Fred Scolari, John Norlander, and "Bones" McKinney. "Red" Auerbach was the player-coach. The game was a highly contested game throughout, but the sailors won by a few points.

After being discharged from the Navy, McKinney became the coach of the Washington Capitols basketball team, and Scolari, Norlander, and McKinney formed the nucleus of the team. The scheduled home games were played at the Uline Area, located at 3rd and M streets in Northeast Washington, DC.

There were other groups and organizations in the area which sponsored their own basketball teams. Some were successful, others were not. One of the more successful teams was one organized and sponsored by Cortez Peters, who became a neighbor of mine when he and his family moved next door in 1946. At that time, we lived in the 3600 block of 11th Street, Northwest. Cortez Peters, who had been recognized as "The World's Fastest Typist," owned and operated the Cortez Peters Business School in the 900 block of U Street, Northwest. Members of his team were amateur players who had played basketball in high school, college, or pickup games on courts in their respective neighborhoods. Nonetheless, his teams were outstanding year after year.

Some of his players were Terry Day, a three-letterman (football, basketball, and baseball) at Armstrong High School and Morgan State College in Baltimore, Maryland; "Greeky" Watson; Weldon Peterson, brother of Jay Peterson who played at Armstrong; Billy Lawton; Holsey Lee, brother of Reggie Lee a three-sport letterman in high school who also played at Armstrong; Ralph "Daddy Grace" Paige, father of star running back Tony Paige from DeMatha, Virginia Tech, and the NFL's New York Jets and the Miami Dolphins; Harry Caldwell, who later played with the world-famous Harlem Globetrotters; and Eugene Littles, a graduate of McKinley Tech and High Point College in North Carolina, a player in the National Basketball League for several seasons, and basketball coach at North Carolina A&T College in Greensboro.

Peters's stepdaughter Sheila, who was "Miss Capital Classic" in 1956, married Willie Wood, a former Armstrong High School great in football, baseball, and basketball. He became a quarterback at Southern California University and later played for the Green Bay Packers. He went on to become an All-Pro Defensive Back in the National Football League (NFL) and a Hall of Famer.

In 1946 almost immediately after the basketball season ended, the baseball season was upon us. Harold Jackson, who was also the public-address announcer for the Washington Homestead Grays, a baseball team in the Negro National League, invited me to accompany him to Griffith Stadium on a day when the Grays were playing. He told me he would see if he could get me a job with the team. When we arrived, he took me into the clubhouse and introduced me to Mr. Dido, the gentleman responsible for all of the Grays' equipment and uniforms. He asked Mr. Dido if he could find a job for me in some capacity with the team. That very day, at the age of fourteen, I became the batboy for the Washington Homestead Grays. The Homestead Grays team was owned by Cumberland Posey and Rufus "Sonny Man" Jackson. They brought the team from Homestead, Pennsylvania, just outside Pittsburgh to play in Griffith Stadium when the Washington Senators (also known as the Washington Nats) were not playing home games. The Senators were not winning many games in those days, and the Grays, who had won their league championship for nine consecutive years from 1937 to 1945, drew larger crowds.

Other teams in the Negro National League were the Baltimore Elite Giants, the Newark Eagles, the New York Black Yankees, the New York Cubans, and the Philadelphia Stars. The other Negro baseball league during that era was the Negro American League, composed of the Birmingham Black Barons, the Chicago American Giants, the Cleveland Buckeyes, the Indianapolis Clowns, the Kansas City Monarchs, and the Memphis Red Sox.

When I was batboy for the Homestead Grays, some of the players on the team and their positions were Vic Harris, Manager; "Candy" Jim Taylor, coach; Walter "Buck" Leonard, first base; "Jelly" Jackson, second base; Sam Bankhead, shortstop; Jud Wilson, third base; Bob Thurman, right field and pitcher; Jerry Benjamin, center field; James "Cool Papa" Bell, left field; Josh Gibson, catcher; Johnny Wright, pitcher; Ray Brown, pitcher; R.T. Walker, pitcher; Frank "Ground Hog" Thompson, pitcher; Dave Hoskins, outfield and pitcher; Wilmer "Red" Fields, third base and pitcher; Howard Easterling, third base; Luis Marquez, second base; Roy Gaston, catcher; Ned Napier, catcher; Luke Easter, outfield and first base; Ray Battle, shortstop and third base; Dave Pope, outfield; Bob Trice, pitcher; and Edward Robinson, infield.

Although this was before integration, the Grays played all-white teams such as the House of David and the Brooklyn Bushwicks. I recall all of the players on the House of David's team wearing beards. This may have been because of their religious beliefs, but at the time, I didn't give it too much thought. I also remember traveling to Brooklyn, New York, with the Grays when they played the Brooklyn Bushwicks in their stadium. My father was not in favor of my traveling to Brooklyn with the team because I was still quite young. But the manager of the team, Mr. Vic Harris, assured my father he would look after me while we were away. Because it was not an overnight trip, my father acquiesced and permitted me to go.

The Grays played single league games at night during the week, usually on Thursdays, and doubleheaders on Sunday afternoon. Occasionally they played twilight-night doubleheaders with two teams from the Negro American League playing against each other in the first game. For example: the Memphis Red Sox would play the Cleveland Buckeyes in the first game. Then in the second game, two teams from the Negro National League, such as the Baltimore Elite Giants and the Homestead Grays, would play. I recall when a twilight-night doubleheader was scheduled between the Birmingham Black Barons and the Kansas City Monarchs, the names of Piper Davis, who played with the Barons, and "Buck" O'Neill and Satchel Paige, who played with the Monarchs, were used in advertising the game to generate more publicity in hopes of drawing a larger crowd for the first game. In the second game between the Philadelphia Stars and the Homestead Grays, Buster Clarkson and Ted "Double Duty" Radcliff were headliners for the Stars and Buck Leonard,

Cool Papa Bell, and Josh Gibson were headliners for the Grays. Satchel Paige didn't show up in time for the first game. Paige was such a drawing card and many of the fans in the stands had come to see him pitch, so when he did arrive, the management let him pitch three innings for the Philadelphia Stars against the Homestead Grays. Satchel Paige pitched three scoreless innings and was relieved by a pitcher for the Philadelphia Stars. I understand he left the stadium immediately and went to the stadium office to pick up his check for his effort. It wasn't too much for the Grays to play a Sunday doubleheader against the Baltimore Elite Giants and immediately afterward travel to Baltimore to play a night game against the Elite Giants.

In July of 1946, the Negro National League All-Stars played the Negro American League All-Stars at Griffith Stadium. At that time, I was privileged to be the batboy for the National League All-Stars. Some of the outstanding players on the National League All-Stars team were Don Newcombe, Larry Doby, and Monte Irvin from the Newark Eagles; James "Junior" Gilliam, Joe Black, and Roy Campanella from the Baltimore Elite Giants; Luis Tiant and Minnie Minoso from the New York Cubans; Buster Clarkson and Ted "Double Duty" Radcliff from the Philadelphia Stars; and James "Cool Papa" Bell, Walter "Buck" Leonard, and Josh Gibson from the Washington Homestead Grays.

Some of the Negro American League All-Stars were Sam Jethroe and Quincy Troupe from the Cleveland Buckeyes; Dan Bankhead from the Memphis Red Sox; Piper Davis from the Birmingham Black Barons; and, "Buck" O'Neill and Satchel Paige from the Kansas City Monarchs.(Jackie Robinson, formerly of the Kansas City Monarchs, had signed to play with the Montreal Royals in October 1945.) There was a lot of excitement in the air that evening. And I was probably as excited as anyone else in the stadium – this was a once-in-a-lifetime event for me.

Some of the players had catchy nicknames, such as "Junior" Gilliam. He was called "Junior" because he was the youngest member of the Baltimore Elite Giants. Ratcliff was nicknamed "Double Duty" because he occasionally started a baseball game as a pitcher and ended up as a catcher. "Cool Papa" got his nickname because he was such a snazzy dresser. He wore a very nice looking suit and color-coordinated the suit with a matching shirt, tie, handkerchief, shoes, socks, and hat. It was also rumored that he was so fast he could cut a wall light switch off and be in bed before the light went out.

I remember Josh Gibson very well. He was very friendly toward me. I recall how he called out my name, "Bil-ly!" He often engaged me in conversation, mostly about baseball. He was a right-handed hitter and all business at the plate. I can envision him pulling his cap down over his head and leaving the top button on his uniform unbuttoned. He took his stance at the plate and methodically took a few practice swings in the pitcher's direction. When Josh connected with the ball it was usually a line drive. I saw him hit many balls into the left-field bleachers at Griffith Stadium, either in practice or during games. Griffith Stadium was 400 feet down the left field line and 420 feet to dead centerfield, making it one of the most difficult places in the Major League to hit a home run. When Josh hit balls, swoosh! It didn't take long for the balls to get out in the bleachers.

Josh brought his son Josh, Jr. down from Pittsburgh occasionally, and we became friends. We played catch on the side of the field and then took the field when the Grays had batting practice. When the games started and one of the Grays' players hit a home run, several of the spectators in the stands got my attention to come over to get dollars from them to give to the players. I was busy collecting money for Josh, Buck Leonard, and, on occasion, Bob Thurman and other members of the team. Josh and Buck hardly needed the dollars. Josh and Buck, along with Satchel Paige, were among the highest paid, if not the highest paid, players in the Negro baseball leagues.

Josh Gibson died in January 1947, and Cumberland Posey and "Sonny Man" Jackson, the owners of the Homestead Grays, went about the task of finding and signing another home-run hitter for their team. They signed Luke Easter, who joined the Grays in the spring of 1947. Luke played the outfield, and when Buck Leonard was not playing, he took Buck's place and played first base. Luke was a big, 6'4", 240-pound, right-handed thrower and left-handed batter. The right-field foul line at Griffith Stadium was 326 feet from home plate to the right-field wall. The right-field wall was 28 feet high, making it difficult for players to hit home runs in that direction. However, Luke hit his share of balls over the wall in batting practice and during games.

The Indianapolis Clowns baseball team played the Grays a couple of times in Griffith Stadium in 1947. They were always a draw in Washington; they mixed their baseball skills with clowning around while they were playing. This, of course, led to a lot of laughter and excitement on the part of the fans. The laughter was generated mainly by two individuals: King Tut, who wore a grass skirt over his baseball uniform and smoked a cigar as he danced the hula and a variety of other dances; and Reece "Goose" Tatum, who played first base for the Clowns. Goose went through a number of gyrations as he caught the ball to put a runner out, again causing roars of laughter from the crowd.

Prior to one of the games between the Clowns and the Grays, I was catching with one of the Grays' players in front of the Grays' dugout. Goose Tatum walked by and noticed the glove I was catching with. My glove was a first-baseman's mitt with a web I had made with cowhide and adhesive tape. Goose asked me if he could catch with it for a few minutes. I took the glove off, handed it to him, and watched him catch for awhile. When he finished, he told me he really liked the glove and asked if I would sell it to him. Right away, I was in awe. I really felt I was on cloud nine. Here was a professional baseball player asking little ole me if I would sell him my first-baseman's mitt. I sold him the glove for six dollars. Although I knew my glove was worth more, I felt honored that he had asked to buy it. Goose Tatum later stopped playing first base for the Indianapolis Clowns and began playing basketball with the world-famous Harlem Globetrotters. He became known as the Clown Prince of Basketball.

In 1947 the Brooklyn Dodgers owner Branch Rickey brought Jackie Robinson up to play with the team. When that happened, it generated a lot of enthusiasm among most of the players in the Negro leagues. Many of them were hoping to get a similar opportunity to move up to the Major Leagues. There seemed to be a euphoric feeling permeating among many of the players. After that, their efforts were more intense. I could see the hustle, determination, focus, and concentration by other ballplayers as they performed on the field.

But times were very difficult for Jackie Robinson as a player with the Dodgers. He received racial insults on and off the baseball field. On the field, opposing players tried to spike him if he was covering a base. Pitchers threw at him and often hit him when he was at bat. Sam Lacy, the sportswriter for the Afro-American newspaper, wrote about the many experiences Jackie encountered on and off the field. Branch Rickey had been very selective in his decision to sign Jackie to play with the Dodgers. He anticipated many of the hardships and problems any player of color would be confronted with as a major-league player and wanted someone with Jackie's character, demeanor, and background. Jackie was a college graduate and had served as an officer in the United States Army.

I entered Dunbar Senior High School in September 1946. Dunbar was a part of the Division II segregated Washington, DC Public School System at that time. Other high schools in the Division II system were Armstrong, Cardozo, and Phelps. Armstrong was a technical high school; Cardozo was a business high school; Phelps was a vocational high school; and Dunbar was an academic high school. Unfortunately, Dunbar was the only school with a stadium (Brooks Stadium) to accommodate football and track. The football teams of all four schools practiced at facilities away from their schools. Armstrong practiced in the Bundy School yard; Cardozo practiced at the Banneker playground area; Phelps practiced in the area across the street from Brown Junior High School; and Dunbar practiced on a lot across from the Northeast Market near Gallaudet College in Northeast Washington.

Cardozo was located at 9th Street and Rhode Island Avenue, Northwest, in the 1940s. In the early 1950s it was moved to the Old Central High School building, which occupied the entire block located between 11th and 13th streets and Florida Avenue and Clifton Street. None of the four high schools had gymnasiums to seat spectators. As a result, games between the schools were played at Turner's Arena. Doubleheader basketball games were usually scheduled on Fridays after school, and a rotating schedule was drawn up so each team played the other team twice. During the 1948-49 basketball season, the basketball games were switched from Turner's Arena, located at 14th and W streets, Northwest, to the National Guard Armory, located at 19th and East Capitol streets, Southeast, where the Robert F. Kennedy Stadium is currently located. The Armory would accommodate more spectators. It also served as the site for indoor track meets.

During my first year at Dunbar, Mr. Charles Pinderhughes was the head football coach. Mr. Pinderhughes had several outstanding football players on his team, players such as Elmer "Buster" Downing, end; Earl "Teddy" Beam, end; Otto Jordan, guard; and John "Jack" Taylor, back. The football team practiced in Brooks Stadium, located behind Dunbar in an area along the track and off the regulation football field outside the track.

Prior to the 1946-47 basketball season, Dunbar was known as the Dunbar Poets, after Paul Lawrence Dunbar, a well-known poet for whom the school had been named. When Mr. Jesse Chase became the basketball coach in 1946, he was responsible for changing the nickname from the Poets to the Dunbar Crimson Tide, by which Dunbar is known today. In 1947 Mr. Chase became the head football coach at Dunbar. Having a new coach on board seemed to inspire a lot of students to come out for the football team. At the first team meeting 125 potential players showed up. Because of the large number of students who came out for the team, a larger practice site was needed. Coach Chase selected the site now occupied by Hamilton Junior High School and Gallaudet College in Northeast Washington. We had to walk there daily for football practice in our practice togs and cleats from Dunbar, located at 1st and M streets, Northwest.

Under Coach Chase's tutelage we used the single wing in which we shifted into the formation. We also used a modified version of the "T" formation which we shifted into as well. However, the quarterback kept his hands on his knees in a semi-upright position, rather than place his hands with fingers spread apart underneath the center's legs.

I was a quarterback on the football team as well as the punter. I recall prior to our last game of the season in 1947, Dunbar was scheduled to play our neighbor, Armstrong, located across the street. On a Monday after school, not thinking that my focus should have been on football and the upcoming game the following Monday, I asked my mother if I could have a party that Friday. She consented. The party was well attended with people nearly wall-to-wall. When we returned to school the following Monday, some of the young ladies told Coach Chase they had attended a great party at Billy Coward's house the previous Friday. When he saw me, he told me without hesitation that I was off the team. He was visibly angry, and it was evident his anger was directed at me for having the party, especially because many of those there were members of the football team.

On the day of the game, I was sitting in the bleachers with my neighbor Elmer Bowman, who is now Dr. Elmer Bowman, D.D.S., watching the game as a punting situation arose for Dunbar. On fourth down Coach Chase sent in Julian Cook to punt. Julian kicked the ball five yards from the line of scrimmage. Julian is currently a retired judge who lives in Detroit. Later in the game another punting situation occurred. This time, Coach Chase sent Chester Walker to punt on fourth down. Chester kicked the ball straight up in the air, to the chagrin of the coach and spectators. Suffice it to say, Armstrong won the football game. To this day, some people think *I* was the punter on both occasions. I was a left-footed punter; both Julian and Chester were right-footed punters, but apparently they had not taken note of this. Unfortunately, Dunbar had a losing season that year against all three of the local high schools – Armstrong, Cardozo, and Phelps.

Nonetheless, the 1947 Dunbar High School football team was quite unique. We had the Chambers brothers on that team. Lawrence Chambers was a senior and a lineman; Andrew was a junior and a back; and, Melvin was a sophomore and a lineman. Lawrence went on to the Naval Academy and became a Rear Admiral. He was Captain on the USS Midway, an aircraft carrier of the US Navy, during the Vietnam War. Andrew, who was captain of the football and baseball teams at Dunbar, enrolled in Howard University after graduation and became captain of the football and baseball teams there as well. As a student, he was commissioned a second lieutenant in the ROTC program. The leadership abilities he displayed through sports served him well as he rose from a second lieutenant in the Army to a lieutenant general.

Several football players on the team went on to outstanding careers: Leander Morgan became the mayor of New Bern, North Carolina; Arnold "Mouse" Webster became the superintendent of schools in Camden, New Jersey, and also mayor of Camden; Elmer Brooks became a general in the US Air Force and served as the missile combat crew commander in Lincoln, Nebraska, during the Cuban Missile Crisis. He appeared in an interview on the television program "60 Minutes" during that time.

During the off-season in 1947, I pleaded with Coach Chase to let me return to the team. My mother also spoke with him on the telephone and also asked that I be allowed to return to the team. After a period of time, he acquiesced and permitted me to return under the condition that I apologize to the team and become a leader by displaying my efforts in conditioning, determination, and attitude.

The 1948 football season began, and I set out to prove that I was an asset to the team. I got my old job back as a punter and also played quarterback, defensive back, and linebacker. I recall having an outstanding game as a linebacker against Cardozo and, throwing a touchdown pass to Elmer Brooks in our last game of the year against Armstrong. Although Dunbar didn't have a very good won/lost record, I thought we had some very good talent on the team. Those who come to mind were Melvin Jones, end; Billy Chinn, guard; John "Jack" Boyd, center; Leander Morgan, end; George Wright, back; Arnold "Mouse" Webster, back; Melvin Spencer, back; Andrew Chambers, back; Tommy Gray, back; James O'Neal, tackle; and Elmer Brooks, end.

Cardozo was the reigning football champions during the middle to late 1940s under the leadership of Coach Sylvester "Sal" Hall. In 1948 they were undefeated, un-scored upon, and untied. Some of the outstanding players on Cardozo's football team during this era were Raymond Carter, end; Russell Williams, guard; Fred Britton, tackle; Benjamin Waddell, guard; Edward Allen, tackle; Maurice "Sonny" Wills, back; Leo Miles, back; and Steve Ellerbe, back.

Armstrong's football players were no slouches either. During the 1940s and early 1950s, Coach Theodore "Ted" McIntyre led Armstrong to many football victories. Some of the outstanding Armstrong athletes who played on the 1948 team were James Walls, tackle; Stanley Gainor, guard; Eugene Smith, back; Avatus Stone, back; Harold Reed, tackle; Arthur Van Brackle, back; Lorenzo White, center; Paul Alexander, end; and Francis Henderson, back. Avatus Stone and I were in the first grade together. "Juice," as he was affectionately known, received a football scholarship to Syracuse University after graduating from Armstrong and later went on to play several seasons in the Canadian Football League. He was an outstanding punter.

The Phelps football teams, coached by Dave Brown during that era, were formidable opponents. Opposing teams knew they were in for a tough game when they played Phelps. Some of the players that performed at a very high level were Ellsworth "Sandy" Freeman, end; Harry "Doc" Franklin, back; James Strivers, center; Francis Lewis, back; and Edward "Mojo" Isley, back.

Almost immediately after football season, we began practice for the 1948-49 basketball season. The Dunbar basketball team was very successful, compiling a record of seventeen wins and four losses. Louis Williams, a native of Kansas and a graduate of Howard University, was our coach. We were successful in defeating all of our opponents whom we played twice with the exception of Armstrong, who defeated us twice that year.

The four high school basketball teams, Armstrong, Dunbar, Cardozo, and Phelps, played doubleheader games at the National Guard Armory, usually on Fridays at 3:30 P.M., and rotated teams on the following Fridays. In a game Dunbar played against Phelps, according to Fred Leigh, a sportswriter for the Afro-American newspaper, "Dunbar's overwhelming victory over Phelps marked the highest scoring contest witnessed among local high schools in the past three years." We beat Phelps by the score of 64 to 39. Elmer Brooks was the leading scorer in the game with 22 points; I was the second highest scorer with 12 points. Kermit Banks and Melvin Jones scored 10 points each. Although I didn't consider myself to be a scorer – I considered myself to be more of a passer, rebounder, and defensive player – I did lead the team in scoring in a game we played against Carver of Baltimore that year, and we won 52-49. I scored 12 points and Kermit Banks was a runner-up with 11 points. The exceptional shooters on the team were Elmer Brooks, Kermit Banks, and Donald Lipscomb. I recall when Donald Lipscomb was brought up from the Junior Varsity team and soon afterward scored 27 points in a game we lost against Dunbar of Baltimore 47-52. Dunbar of Baltimore was coached by "Sugar" Cain, a former basketball player for Morgan State College and the Washington Lichtman Bears professional basketball team, who was renowned for his exceptional basketball skills.

At the end of our regular season, we traveled to Fayetteville State College in North Carolina to participate in a high school basketball tournament. Unfortunately, we came up short, losing in the first round. Armstrong also participated and won the tournament.

As I recently looked at a photograph of the 1948-49 Dunbar of Washington basketball team, I realized what a remarkable group of young men they were. Every one of them graduated from Dunbar and went on to college. Among these players, three of them rose to the rank of general in the military. I have previously mentioned two of these young athletes: Elmer Brooks and Andrew Chambers. Elmer, who was an end on the football team and captain on the basketball team, became a brigadier general in the Air Force. Andrew, who was a captain on the football team, became a lieutenant general in the Army. The third athlete, Hugh Robinson, enrolled in West Point and became a second lieutenant in the Army. Hugh quickly moved up through the ranks, was assigned to be a military aide to President Lyndon B. Johnson, and ultimately became a major general. Others became teachers, school administrators, lawyers, real estate agents, high school or college coaches, and physicians, among other professions.

The other three high schools in the city also produced phenomenal athletes and coaches. Armstrong High School was the outstanding basketball team in the Inter-High Division II during the late 1940s and 1950s. They were led by a remarkable coach, Charles "Charlie" Baltimore. In 1948-49 they won the city championship and the South Atlantic High School Athletic Conference Championship. Some of their more prominent players were Paul Alexander, who later in life became a very good tennis player; John Hobbs; Leslie Morgan; Eugene Lawrence, who was the leading scorer on the team; Thomas "Rip" Spencer, who later played for the world-famous Harlem Globetrotters; Avatus Stone; and Jay Peterson, who after graduation from Armstrong attended my alma mater, North Carolina College, on a basketball scholarship.

In 1948-49, Cardozo was coached by Don Porter. During that season, we at Dunbar were fortunate to win both games against them. Some of the better-known Cardozo players on that team were Samuel Moore, William Whitington, Steve Ellerbe, Herman "Stump" Baylor, and Leo Miles, who attended Virginia State College (now Virginia State University) in Petersburg, Virginia, and later played professional football with the New York Giants.

During the 1948-49 school year, there were several very good athletes in the Inter-High who participated in three sports and received letters in each of the three sports. I thought this was a tremendous feat. Each of them had to maintain a "C" average or better in each of their classes and was required to practice and to play in the sports of their choosing. Among the three-lettermen from Cardoza were Steve Ellerbe, Maurice "Maury" Wills, Leo Miles, and Herman "Stump" Baylor. Each lettered in football, basketball, and baseball. Those from Armstrong were Avatus Stone, Reggie Lee, and Paul Alexander. Stone and Lee lettered in the three major high-school sports of that era while, in addition to basketball and football, Alexander lettered in tennis. At Dunbar, the three lettermen were Andrew Chambers, football, basketball, and baseball; Theodore Hill, basketball, football, and track; and me, Billy Coward, football, basketball, and baseball.

There have been many excellent players groomed and coached in the high schools in Washington, DC who have come before and after those mentioned here. One of those who come to mind is Garrett "Gary" Mays. Gary, an exceptional basketball player, was coached by Charles Baltimore during the 1951-54 basketball seasons at Armstrong Technical High School. Gary was born in Verwell, West Virginia, and had lost his left arm in a shotgun accident when he was about five years old. He came to Washington when he was twelve. I recall seeing Gary for the first time when we were swimming at the Banneker Swimming Pool as teenagers.

Gary did not let the fact that he had only one arm impede his love for sports or his ability to participate. He performed in basketball and baseball much better than many other individuals I have seen play with two arms. He was very agile and swift of foot. He was very competitive and confident in his ability to excel. He was always upbeat whenever I saw him. Gary is a shining example for all of us, those with and without physical handicaps. When I think of Gary, I think of the saying "Don't let what you cannot do interfere with what you can do." He has served and continues to serve as an inspiration and motivational force to all who have known him.

There were other young men who played sports in the DCPS who also deserve recognition. During the 1952-53 basketball season, Phelps Vocational High School's basketball team was coached by Lieutenant Dave Brown. Among the players on the team were Walter "Rock" Greene, Maxwell Banks, and Elgin "Rabbit" Baylor. Rock Greene was a three-sport athlete participating in football, basketball, and baseball. He went to Delaware State College in Dover, Delaware, on an athletic scholarship. He has since been enshrined in the Delaware State Hall of Fame. Upon graduation, he became a teacher and a successful basketball coach at his high school alma mater. He also became a basketball referee.

Maxwell Banks later went on to Hollywood, changed his name to Max Julian, and made several movies. He played the starring role in the movie *Bushrod and Cleopatra*. Maxwell's brother, Tazewell Banks, is currently a retired cardiologist, avid swimmer, and frequent participant in the Senior Olympics.

The following year, 1953-54, Lieutenant Brown moved to Spingarn High School and became the basketball coach. Elgin Baylor, or "Rabbit" as we called him, transferred to Spingarn from Phelps to again play for Coach Brown. With coaching from Brown and excellent efforts from Rabbit, Spingarn was undefeated during the regular basketball season. Spingarn had played Armstrong twice during the regular season and defeated them on both occasions. Rabbit scored 40 some points in each game. Armstrong met Spingarn again that year in the Inter-High Division II Basketball Tournament. Armstrong's coach, Charlie Baltimore, designed a box-and-one defense to help curtail the shooting of Rabbit, with Gary Mays and his quick feet following Rabbit all over the court. With that defense, Gary held Rabbit to 18 points and Armstrong won the game. Gary was captain of Armstrong's team during the 1953-54 basketball season.

During the 1954 Inter-High baseball season, Gary, who played catcher, was selected as captain of the Armstrong baseball team. It was truly amazing he could perform on the baseball field as he did with one arm. Against an Inter-High team with a man on first base for the opposing team, the runner on first base attempted to steal second base as the Armstrong pitcher pitched to the next batter. Gary caught the ball from the pitcher and threw the ball in the air. While the ball was in the air, he put his catcher's mitt under his left arm and caught the ball as it came down and then threw the runner out before the runner reached second base. (Gary is shown in the picture of the New Cage outfit semi-pro basketball team with jersey 7, kneeling, second from the right.)

In the mid-1950s two outstanding athletes were evolving in the Inter-High schools. One was Willie Wood, who attended Armstrong. He was a three-sport athlete having played football, basketball, and baseball. He was a versatile quarterback on the football team. Upon graduation from Armstrong, he attended a junior college and then enrolled in the University of Southern California where he played quarterback and defensive back. He was not drafted by any of the NFL teams but got a tryout with the Green Bay Packers. He made the Packers team as a defensive back and played for a total of nine years with the team. He played in eight Pro Bowls and Super Bowls I and II. After his playing days were over, he was an assistant coach with the San Diego Chargers, head coach of the Toronto Argonauts in the Canadian Football League, and head coach of the Philadelphia Bell of the former World Football League. Willie was inducted into the NFL's Hall of Fame on August 5, 1989.

I had known Willie for a number of years but got to know him better years later during his football career with the Green Bay Packers. During the off-season in the spring of 1967, Willie invited me to work out with him. He told me he had a new exercise gadget called an Exer-Genie, which Vince Lombardi got for all of the members of the Green Bay Packers football team. It was mandatory that they use this piece of equipment during the football season and after the season was over; Lombardi wanted all of his players to stay in good condition year round.

Willie came by my house one day to show me the Exer-Genie. To demonstrate it for me, we went across the street from my home to a large playground area behind Coolidge High School and next to the football field and track. Willie attached the gadget to a backstop used for softball and went through a series of exercises intended to build strength, endurance, and increasing flexibility. The Exer-Genie is an isometric and isotonic exerciser. After Willie demonstrated an exercise, he let me use the Exer-Genie to perform the same exercise. I was so impressed with the equipment that I told my friend Leo Miles about it. He in turn told Mr. Charles Baltimore, the principal at Bell Vocational High School about it. Leo was coaching at Bell. He asked for permission to purchase ten Exer-Genies for the football team. Ten stations were set up for the football team to utilize and develop different muscle groups. The Exer-Genie can be used to enhance muscle development in a variety of sports, such as football, basketball, baseball, bowling, track, tennis, wrestling, swimming, and golf.

The other player of note in the mid-1950s was Willie Jones, who played basketball and baseball at Dunbar. He was an outstanding player, a tremendous competitor, and a very, very confident basketball player. Willie was known throughout the Washington area in school gyms and on playgrounds for his playing ability and his trash-talking to his opponents. He went on to play basketball at American University and played exceptionally well. During this period, he received any number of accolades for his performances on the basketball court. Many years later his jersey was retired and hung in the rafters of American University's Bender Arena, along with Kermit Washington's jersey, in a ceremony I was privileged to attend. After college graduation, Willie played professionally with the Washington Tapers.

I frequently find that high school football, basketball, and baseball officials who have distinguished themselves with their knowledge about the rules and regulations of these three sports are not acknowledged in periodicals or books written about the subject. Because of this, it is my intention to acknowledge and to identify some of these officials throughout this book. Some of the men who officiated at the Washington, DC Inter-High games (football, basketball, or baseball) during that era were Ralph Garner, "Bus" Tinnen, Otis Troupe, Biff Carter, William Rumsey, and Joseph "Joe" Drew.

Otis Troupe was an outstanding football player at Morgan State College, making the All-CIAA (Colored Intercollegiate Athletic Association, later renamed the Central Intercollegiate Athletic Association), football team. He later became a police officer in Washington, DC. "Bus" Tinnen was a teacher in the DC Public School System, Division II. Ralph Garner was an employee with the DC Department of Recreation. Biff Carter was a teacher and coach at Phelps Vocational High School and later became an aide to US Congressman John Conyers. William Rumsey was principal of McKinley Tech High and became the director of the DC Recreation Department. Joe Drew was also a teacher in the DC Public School System, Division II. Joe was the brother of Dr. Charles Drew, the first person to develop the blood bank, and the uncle of Charlene Drew Jarvis, a former member of the Washington, DC City Council.

Phelps was a formidable opponent for Dunbar. Not only did Phelps have very good basketball players, but their coach, Dave Brown, was nicknamed "The Fox" because of his shrewd basketball strategies, game after game. Whenever a team played the Tradesmen, as they were also known, you could expect tough competition. In one of the two games in which we played against Phelps, they played as though they had not quite warmed up – their shots were not falling. It seemed as if there was an invisible cover over the basket. On the other hand, our team was hot. Shots were falling from various angles all over the basketball court for us.

Some of the players on Phelps' team were Alvin Winestock, who was usually their leading scorer, Harry "Doc" Franklin, Ellsworth "Sandy" Freeman, Gilbert "Kid" Jackson, and Eugene Goodall.

Some of the basketball referees who officiated our games were Harry Woods; Herman "Bud" Tyrance, who taught at Howard University and later became head of the physical education department at Howard; and John Burr, who taught at Howard and preceded Herman Tyrance as head of the physical education department and for whom the John H. Burr Gymnasium at Howard is named; Otis Troupe; Bus Tinnen; Joseph "Joe" Drew; and James Wyatts.

At the end of the basketball season, we went almost immediately into the baseball season. Our baseball coach that year was Leslie R. Simms. Because we lacked a practice facility, the baseball team encountered the same problem as the football team; we had to walk from Dunbar at 1st and M streets, Northwest, to the practice site located near the 6th Street market and Galludet College in Northeast Washington. We had the nucleus of a pretty good baseball team, particularly on the defensive side of the team. Frank Phillips played several positions – pitcher, shortstop, and catcher; I played first base; Lawrence "Punchy" Robinson, second base; Willis Johnson, shortstop and second base; Chester Walker, outfield and right field; Eugene "Biddy" Tapscott, second base and pitcher; Lorenzo Jackson, catcher and left field; Andrew Chambers, centerfield; George Wright centerfield; Freddy Johnson, outfield; and Clifford Smith, pitcher. Of course, the positions played depended on who Coach Simms chose for the starting lineup and what positions he wanted individuals to play for a particular game.

Frank Phillips had a very strong throwing arm. He was an exceptional baseball player, whether catching or playing shortstop. I recall when we were playing a game (I don't remember who our opponents were at the time), a situation came up when the other team was at bat and Dunbar was in the field. One of the batsmen got on first base by a walk. I was playing first base and thought the other team would attempt to get the next batter to lay down a bunt to advance the runner on first base to second base. So I called all of the infielders to the pitcher's mound and told Phillips to call for a pitchout away from home plate. Eugene Tapscott was the pitcher. I told them that just before Tapscott pitched the ball, I would leave the runner on first base and start running toward home plate, looking for a bunt. As I approached home plate, the runner on first base started toward second base. Tapscott threw the pitchout to the side of home plate to Phillips. And Phillips threw the ball to Willis Johnson, the shortstop, who tagged the runner out at second base. After that play took place, the other team did not score, and we came off the field for our turn at bat. Coach Simms asked what the conversation at the pitcher's mound was about, and Phillips told him I had called for the pitchout and it worked. Coach Simms lit up in a big smile.

Playing outfield in that game were: Lorenzo Jackson in left field, when he wasn't catching; Andy Chambers in centerfield; and George Wright in right field. Chambers had a wide range, and not too many baseballs got by him because of his speed. He was also a good hitter and a switch hitter, meaning that he batted right-handed or left-handed. Chambers, along with Johnson, Phillips, Walker, and Jackson, formed the nucleus of the team's hitting or offensive power. In 1949 we had a record of 6 wins and 4 losses.

Cardozo, coached by Don Porter, also had a respectable baseball team during that season. Some of their better players were Herman "Stump" Baylor, third base; "Lefty" Cleveland Edwards, pitcher; Carl "Dopey" Goings, outfield; Raymond Carter, outfield; Steve Ellerbe, second base; Leo Miles, catcher; and Maurice "Maury" Wills, shortstop and pitcher. Maury Wills later moved up through the Minor League Baseball system and into the Major Leagues to play shortstop for the Los Angeles Dodgers. While playing for the Dodgers from 1960 to 1965, he led the team and Major League in stolen bases. He was named the National League's Most Valuable Player in 1962.

I would be remiss if I did not mention some of the exceptional players who were members of Armstrong's 1949 baseball team. They were John Hobbs, third base; Louis Jackson, first base; Arthur Van Brackle, second base; Haywood Mims, pitcher; Alvatus Stone, catcher; and Reggie Lee, pitcher.

Phelps, coached by Dave "The Fox" Brown, was always very competitive in baseball in those days. Several of their outstanding players were Benjamin Jones, third base; Milton Gross, shortstop; Francis Lewis, outfield; James Braxton, outfield; and Edward "Mojo" Isley, pitcher. In a game between Dunbar and Phelps in 1949 at the baseball field adjacent to the National Guard Armory at 19th and East Capitol streets, I came up to bat against pitcher Mojo Isley. Isley wasn't the largest player on the Phelps team – in fact, he was one of the smallest. However, he was one of the best pitchers in the Inter-High. He had a big motion in his delivery and a very strong arm. Otis Troupe was officiating behind the plate. Isley threw a pitch to me which I thought was a fastball, and the pitch came straight at my head. I ducked out of the way and hit the ground. I thought the pitch was a ball, but when I got up and looked at the umpire, he was smiling and holding his right hand and finger up, indicating a strike. Isley had thrown one of the sharpest breaking curves I had ever seen. He went on to pitch and struck me out.

Over 168,000 Fans in 8 Years
1942—18,000 saw Kentucky State Top North Carolina College 21-6
1943—13,000 saw Morgan Raid Florida A&M., 50-0
1944—22,500 saw TAAF Take Morgan, 2-0
1945—18,000 saw TAAF Beat North Carolina College, 14-0
1946—21,000 saw North Carolina College Upset Tennessee State, 14-6
1947—24,000 saw Tenn. State Top West Virginia State, 27-13
1948—25,000 saw West Virginia State Raid Virginia State, 18-2
1949—30,000 saw West Virginia State Lash North Carolina College, 14-0

B. Coward's Personal Collection

A HISTORY IN PHOTO OF

The Greatest Grid Spectacle In the History of Minority Football .. The

CAPITAL CLASSIC

1942 - 1948

(Right) Joe Thompkins, Va State, Co-Captain

Ric Roberts, (left) A Steel Bowl, Orange and Peach Blossom Classic founder, caame to D.C. from Atlanta in 1941 and "sold" J. E. "Jerry" Coward, (right) the idea of foot-extravaganza for the District's fans who were in need of recreational outlet.
When Coward said, "I have the right man," he meant C. C. Coley (center) one of the nation's top individual employers of colored folk - and Coward's lifetime friend.
Mr. Coley, an outstanding citizen, invited Milburn F. Wainright, (extreme right) to join four-man team. Put up first $5,000 - in front.

THE CAPITAL CLASSIC STORY

. *by AL SWEENEY*

The saga of the Capital Classic, which tonight celebrates its seventh "birthday", is a tale of men with ingenuity, daring, and loyalty combined with unswerving faith in the adage "if you give the public what they want they will support you."

The name, the idea, the spectacle and all of the ingredients, which blend to make this grid contest "the greatest football show on earth" are all the brainchildren of one man.

That man, a distinguished journalist, who ranks among the finest sportswriters of the nation, regardless of color, is Eric B. (Ric) Roberts.

Ric, whose by-line has long been familiar with sporting page followers for nearly a score of years, came to the District of Columbia during 1941 from Atlanta, Ga., where he had been an ace reporter, cartoonist and picture layout editor for the *Atlanta Daily World*.

In leaving Atlanta, Roberts left behind an amazing array of achievements. He had attended Clark University, where he starred for four years on the greatest eleven ever turned out at the institution. He was a member of Clark's eleven, coached by Sam Taylor, that shattered Tuskegee's phenomenal winning streak of 49 straight games.

After finishing his star-studded all around, three-lettered athletic career with Clark, Roberts joined the staff of the World, where he gained fame as a writer. His colorful writings were responsible for the athletic aggregations

B. Coward's Personal Collection

Capital Classic Programs over the years…

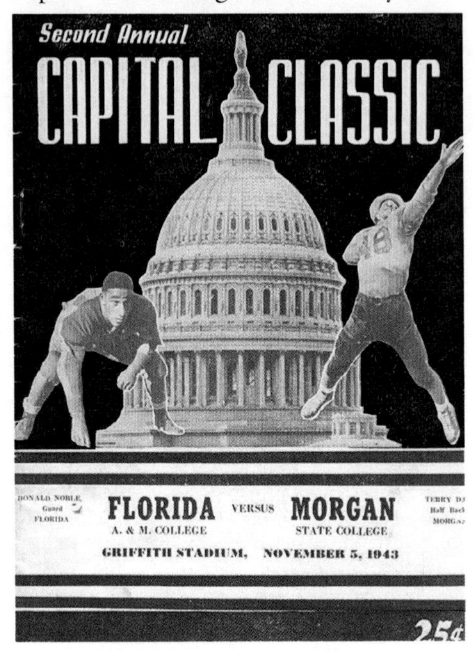

B. Coward's Personal Collection

B. Coward's Personal Collection

B. Coward's Personal Collection

B. Coward's Personal Collection

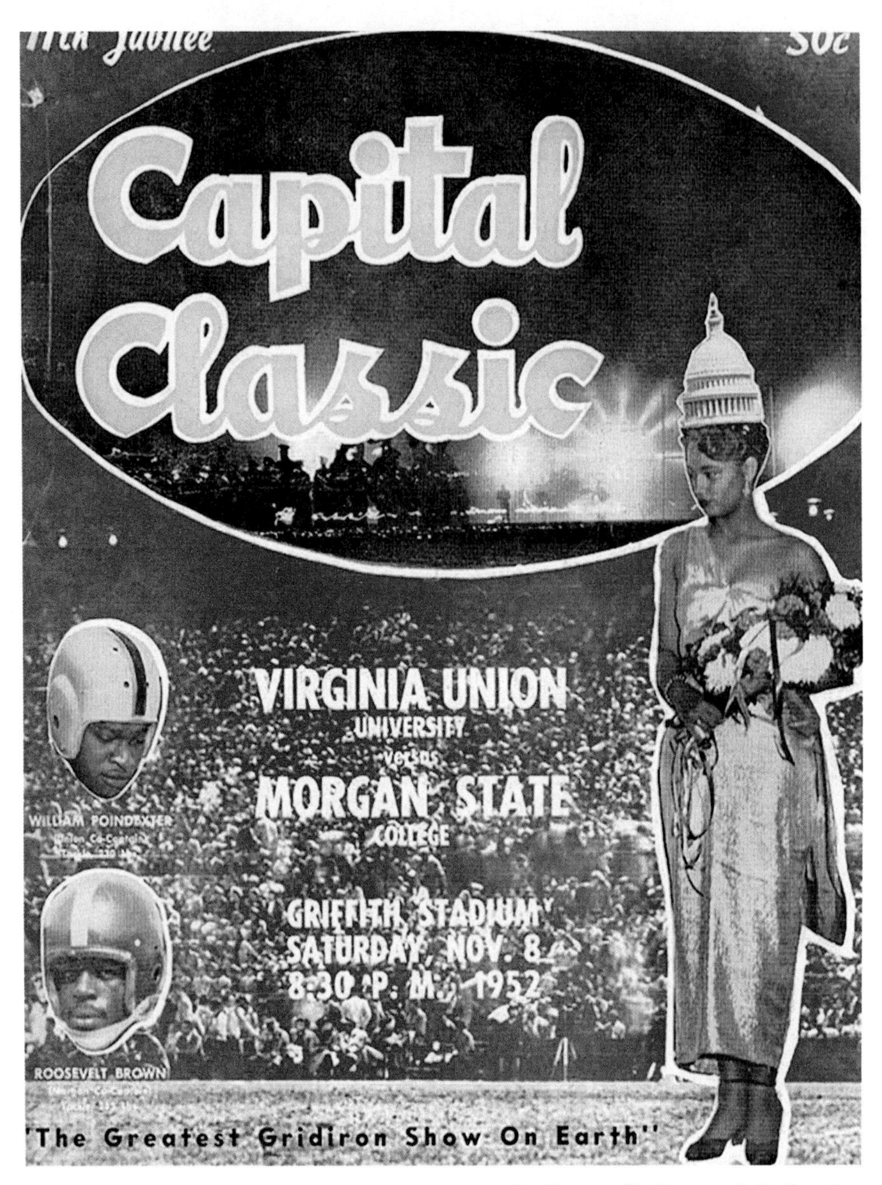

B. Coward's Personal Collection

Photo by F. Turner

Billy Coward's parents, John E. "Jerry" Coward and Thelma Avant Coward, in 1945.

Photo by F. Turner

The Garnet Patterson Lightweight Junior High School City Championship 1945-46 Basketball Team

Seated left to right: R. Scott, Thurmond Long, Leon White, Billy Coward, Arthur Van Brackle
Standing left to right: William Lee, Coach Van Harris, William Whittington
Not pictured Donald Harrington and Thomas Jolly.

Photo by F. Turner

Billy Coward displaying the Walker Memorial Medal awarded to him at his graduation from Garnet Patterson Junior High School in 1946, as the outstanding athlete in school.

Art Carter Papers, Moorland – Spingarn Research Center, Howard University

1946 Washington Homestead Grays from left to right: Jelly Jackson, Ray Battle, Edward Robinson, Sam Bankhead, Josh Gibson, Buck Leonard, Dave Hoskins, Jerry Benjamin, Cool Papa Bell.

P. Covington Photo

Homestead Grays' Luke Easter being congratulated by Wilmer Fields and batboy Billy Coward after he hit a home run at Griffith Stadium, 1947.

Hubbard Photo

Dunbar High School players Billy Coward and Tommy Gray practice punting before a game at Dunbar as teammates James O'Neal and Melvin Jones look on, 1948.

Hubbard Photo

Billy Coward Quarterback for Dunbar, 1948.

Hubbard Photo

Dunbar High School Basketball Team 1948-49, 17 Wins, 4 Losses
Kneeling left to right: Oliver Thompson, Kermit Banks, Melvin Jones, Elmer Brooks, Billy Coward, Andrew Chambers, Donald Lipscomb
Standing left to right: Leotis Burton, Herbert Muriel, James Grant, Coach Lois Williams, Hugh Robinson, James Houston, Louis Ivey

Photo by Harriet Hoover Brown
Hugh Robinson (16), Elmer Brooks (15), and Billy Coward (14) in action at a game played at Banneker 1949.

Chapter 3

UPON GRADUATION FROM Dunbar High School in June 1949, I was fortunate to follow my brother, Leon, to North Carolina College in Durham, North Carolina, on a football scholarship. My brother had also received a football scholarship from 1945 through 1949. However, by the time I arrived at NCC, he had graduated.

The first of September was usually the date we began football preseason practice. I was a young seventeen-year-old college student just out of high school. I remember that over one hundred individuals came out to practice after we finished our physical examinations. Many of the individuals were a few years older than I. During World War II and the Korean Conflict in the 1940s and 1950s, all males in the United States had to register for the draft as soon as they became eighteen. Several of the players who showed up for practice had been in the military. They had been discharged and were attending college on the GI Bill.

I recall vividly how we had to get up at five in the morning before the sun came up to begin a three-mile run out to the railroad track and back. Afterward, we showered, ate breakfast, and briefly relaxed before we had to be on the practice field in our practice football togs ready to go at 9:30 A.M. Practice usually lasted until 11:30 A.M. After practice, we showered again, went to lunch, and then had a short period of rest time in our dormitory rooms before going back to practice at 3:00 P.M. and usually lasting two to two and a half hours. We hit the showers again before going to dinner in the campus dining hall. After dinner we had a team meeting, and then back to our dorms until the next day. This routine was repeated each day except

Sundays for a two-week period before all of the students came back from summer vacation and classes began.

North Carolina College was a member of the CIAA. Other members of the CIAA during that era were Delaware State College of Dover, Delaware; Morgan State College of Baltimore, Maryland; West Virginia State College of Institute, West Virginia; Howard University of Washington, DC; Virginia State College of Petersburg, Virginia; Virginia Union of Richmond, Virginia; Saint Augustine College of Raleigh, North Carolina; Shaw University of Raleigh, North Carolina; Hampton Institute of Hampton, Virginia; Johnson C. Smith College of Charlotte, North Carolina; and North Carolina Agricultural and Technical of Greensboro, North Carolina.

I initially started out as a quarterback, punter, and defensive halfback on the football team. While playing quarterback, my teammates and coaches thought I was very deceptive by faking and handing off the football – so much so that they didn't know who had the ball in our scrimmages. I was showing up very well offensively, but I wasn't getting very much game playing time. This was very frustrating to me because I believed I could play football at that level. I thought about transferring to another school. I was the quarterback for the scout team, running the other team's plays against the defensive team's first unit. And I was very successful in completing passes, faking handoffs, and running the ball against our defensive first team.

I received a letter from another college. The team captain and my former roommate, Butler "Blue Juice" Taylor, picked it up from the college post office, along with mail for other members of the football team, and delivered it. He was aware of my discontent with my lack of playing time. He brought the mail back to the dormitory and delivered it as usual, but I later found out that he had told the coach, Herman Riddick, I had received a letter from another college. After our last game against North Carolina A&T, which we lost, Coach Riddick told me he was coming up to Washington, DC to see the Redskins play the Cleveland Browns and I could come along if I wanted. The Browns were coached by Paul Brown and featured such outstanding players as Otto Graham, Marion Motley, John Wooten, Bill Willis, and Horace Gilliam, among others. During the trip to DC, he told me I would be the starting quarterback in the next season and I would receive a school letter, a jacket, and a trophy for contributing most to the development of the team at the upcoming athletic banquet. But even before the athletic banquet, one of the assistant coaches, Angie Lawrence, gave me the trophy and jacket right after football season was over. Incidentally, Angie Lawrence later became a very good and entertaining basketball official in the CIAA.

During the spring of 1951, the football team was busy with our two-week scheduled training session. At this time the coaches were busy conditioning us with a variety of exercises and a lot of running. We practiced fundamentals, plays, and the execution of plays for each position on the team daily. I played quarterback on offense and safety on defense. During that time, many of the football players played on both offense and defense.

I remember one fellow teammate, Bill Hollingsworth, who did all the kicking off for the team. He was drafted into the Army, and Coach Riddick had several fellows on the team try out to see who would succeed him. I tried out, and although I had never kicked off before but had punted in high school, I won the job as kickoff player. I did all the kicking off for the team for the next two years, my junior and senior years in college.

At the end of spring training, we always scrimmaged and had a lot of physical contact to see how well we could perform and who was really improving. I was playing defensive safety during a scrimmage, and I intercepted a pass intended for Ernie Warlick, our big 6'3", 225-pound starting end. I was returning the interception when I was confronted by Fred Ponder, a tackler and fullback on the offense. I lowered my head as I was about to make contact with him when Ernie Warlick jumped on my back to tackle me, and I fell on my right shoulder. The impact and the added weight of Warlick on my back injured my shoulder. As a result, I could not throw any more passes during my college career. Because of my inability to throw, I could no longer play quarterback, so I switched to running back offensively and continued to play safety on defense.

During the 1951 football season, my junior year, we were tied for first place with West Virginia State College in the CIAA and had gone to Institute, West Virginia, to play them on their home field. I played the entire game on defense as a safety but kicked off only once at the beginning of the game. I remember that game like it was yesterday because of the intensity of the game. Both teams played a very defensive game. When the officials gave the two-minute warning before the game ended, West Virginia had possession of the ball on their 9-yard line deep in their own territory. They ran one play and fumbled the football. NCC recovered on their 7-yard line, and the officials said the game was over. Coach Riddick confronted the referee and asked how the game could be over after only one play and only seconds after the two-minute warning had been called. The referee again ruled the game to be over. The score was West Virginia 0 and North Carolina College 0. We should have had time to run at least three plays or even kick a field goal, but we didn't have a chance to do either.

Our next game was against our archrival, North Carolina A&T in Greensboro, North Carolina, on Thanksgiving Day. We outplayed the Aggies during most of the game. I again played safety during the entire game and kicked off twice, once when the game started and once after we scored a touchdown. At halftime, the score was tied at 6-all. Each team had scored a touchdown but failed to make the extra point. The score was still tied late into the fourth quarter. With less than 3 minutes to play in the game, A&T scored again and kicked the extra point to take a 13-6 lead as time ran out, and the game was over. Statistically, we outplayed A&T in all phases of the game except the one that counted the most: the final score.

Back on campus the following Monday, Coach Riddick held a meeting with the team. The A&T game was the final game on our schedule for the season, and we would normally be turning all of our football equipment in to the equipment manager. Coach Riddick stated that he had received an invitation for the NCC football team to play against the Florida A&M Rattlers in December in the Orange Blossom Classic in the Orange Bowl Stadium in Miami, Florida. He asked if we wanted to accept the invitation. Many of those who spoke up were upperclassmen and those who had played the most during the year. The overriding response was we were tired and, at that point, very disappointed with the outcome of the last two games. We had played West Virginia to a 0-0 tie at West Virginia. Going into that game, we were tied for first place in the CIAA. We then lost to NC A&T in the last minutes of the game, which allowed West Virginia to virtually back into the championship. The team was obviously disappointed and those who spoke out expressed, without reservation, their disappointment and reluctance to participate in the Orange Bowl. Coach Riddick decided to take a vote by a show of hands. A large percentage of the players voted not to go, but Coach Riddick overruled the team and decided to accept the invitation to play anyway.

Most of the fellows on the team had never been to Florida, including myself, so it would be a new experience for many of us. We boarded a bus on campus and went to Raleigh to board the Silver Meter Train on the Seaboard Railroad Line. It took us twelve hours or more to get to Miami. After arriving, we stayed at a place called the Harlem Square. The location of the hotel reminded me of the busy intersection at 7th and T streets in

Northwest Washington, DC. It was quite busy. People were milling about on foot, and the traffic was rather heavy. After checking into our rooms, we were told we would have practice in two hours.

We boarded a bus and practiced at a local high school. It seemed that the effort of many of the players was somewhat lackluster. Our hearts and minds were not into it. After practice, we returned to the hotel and found out there were only two bathrooms for the guests in the entire hotel, so arrangements had to be made for us to take our showers at the new Lord Calvert Motel, where Florida A&M's football team was staying.

The next day, we arrived at the Orange Bowl Stadium and began our pre-game exercises and drills, allowing us to become more familiar with our surroundings. I noticed that Florida A&M had dressed enough football players to line up from one end of the football field to the other. Florida had won the pre-game coin toss to see which team would kick off and which team would receive first. The Rattlers elected to receive first. I kicked off deep into their territory and ran down the field to make the opening tackle of the game. I tackled the ball carrier on Florida's 9-yard line. On the next play, from my position as safety on defense, I chased number 88 down the far sidelines and knocked him out of bounds on our 2-yard line. The player was so fast he reminded me of the Rocket 88 Oldsmobile car that came out about that time. Florida A&M went on to trounce us soundly in the 1951 Orange Bowl Classic. I felt humiliated by the final score, so I won't mention it here. The next day, the *Miami Daily News* ran a picture of me closing in on the runner and driving him out of bounds on the 2-yard line. They scored on the next play.

The following day, we boarded a train on the Seaboard Railway to return to Raleigh. The trip back took us eighteen hours; it seemed that the train stopped every hour. I found out later that the Seaboard Railway system was a single-track system and the train we were on was a local train making frequent stops in small towns to pick up some passengers and let others off. The train also had to pull over to a sidetrack to let express trains and freight trains by. In one instance, the train stopped by an orange grove. Most of the fellows, including myself, had never seen oranges growing before. While the train was stopped, a couple of them foolishly decided to get off the train to pick a few oranges. Shortly afterward the train began to move, and you should have seen them scurrying back to get on the train. Those of us who were on the train watching this scenario were in hysterics. We finally arrived back in Raleigh and boarded a bus back to campus. Our trip to the Orange

Bowl as well as the dismal outcome of the overall trip to Florida, was one experience that has remained very vividly with me all these years.

But my college life was not all football and academics; it was during this time that I met the young lady who was to become my future wife. I noticed her one late afternoon after football practice as I stopped to watch the majorette squad practicing, but it was not until I saw her leaving the cafeteria later that I had an opportunity to say hello. As was the tradition on campus, the football players sat on the rail outside the cafeteria after dinner to joke and kid around as well as to see and be seen. As she passed, I said, "Hello." She seemed a bit shy but returned my greeting. We struck up a conversation, and I found out she was a freshman from Winston-Salem, NC. She had been a majorette in high school as well, but she had also played on the girls' varsity basketball team for three years. It was great to know we had something in common. Unfortunately, girls did not have an opportunity to play college basketball at NCC during that era because the school did not have a girls' varsity basketball team, or any other varsity sports for girls.

The fall of 1952 was the beginning of my senior year and the last football season of my college career. Coach Riddick again had me kicking off in all of the games and playing defense in most of the games. During that season, we were scheduled to play Tennessee State on their home field in Nashville, Tennessee. We took a chartered airplane flight to Nashville for the game. It was the first airplane flight for me and other members of the team. The airplane had two propeller-driven engines, and when we hit an air pocket, the plane dropped suddenly causing, some very anxious moments and concerns among the passengers. We played Tennessee State on an even keel throughout the game. They scored a touchdown and we followed suit. This continued throughout most of the game until the end when we failed to kick two extra points. The final score was Tennessee 28, NCC 26.

In 1952 we played Virginia State College in the National Classic in Griffith Stadium in, Washington, DC. Virginia State was coached by Sylvester "Sal" Hall, who had previously coached Cardozo High School in Washington, DC, during the 1940s but left to coach Virginia State in 1949. As the head coach at Virginia State, he recruited heavily among the high schools in the DC area. Many of the players, whom I played football with or against in high school, enrolled at Virginia State after graduation, and I found myself playing against them when NCC played VSC. Some of the players from Cardozo on the VSC team during that time were Leo Miles,

Steve Ellerbe, Robert Wills (Maury Wills's brother), Ed Allen, Russell Williams, and Rudolph "Lang" McGoins. Those from Armstrong were Clint Freeman and James Coles. My former teammates at Dunbar, whom I played against at VSC, were James O'Neal and James Grant.

North Carolina College played Virginia State in football 4 consecutive times from 1949 through 1952. We were successful in defeating them for 3 straight years in 1949, 1950, and 1951. They finally defeated us in 1952.

I recall the first time in the history of either school that NCC played Maryland State College (now Maryland Eastern Shore, a part of the University of Maryland system). It was 1952, and Maryland State had not yet become a member of the CIAA. At the time, Maryland State was coached by Vernon "Skip" McCain. I remember kicking off to them in the game on the opening play and running down the field to make the tackle on a player who was returning the kickoff. I felt a player on the opposing team brush-block me to impede me from getting to the kickoff return man. Nonetheless, I was still able to focus on the return man, and just as I was about to tackle him, someone blocked me from my blind side and – BOOM! – my lights went out. Later on in the game I kicked off again, and the same thing happened. Just as I was about to make the tackle on the kickoff return man, someone hit me again from my blind side for the second time and – BOOM! – my lights went out again. The next time I kicked off, I cautiously tipped down the field and watched as one of my teammates made the tackle.

After that game was over, I saw one of my homeboys, Cohen Cosby, who incidentally went to Cardozo and ran track and played football. I told him they had really put a hurting on me during the kickoffs. He said they had scouted us in four prior games with other schools and I had made a tackle after I had kicked off in each of the games. So, their coach, Vernon McCain, devised a play especially to prevent me from making a tackle on the kickoff.

At another time, as we were dressing for a game against Johnson C. Smith College in Charlotte, North Carolina, Coach Riddick came up to me and asked if I was ready to play some defense. I told him I wanted to play some offense because I had been playing offense against his first-team defensive unit when we scrimmaged and had been running all over them when I carried the ball. In that game we were favored over JC Smith by three touchdowns. Going into the last few minutes of the first half the score was tied 0-0. Coach Riddick called me to go into the game to play halfback on offense. I was effective in gaining ten and fifteen yards a clip, leading to a touchdown run by Fred McNeil. After faking a handoff to me as the half ended, with NCC taking a 7-0 halftime lead, we won the game 14-0.

The last two games of the season were against West Virginia State College and North Carolina A&T. Although NCC came up on the short end of the score against West Virginia (14-7) and A&T (13-6), we were very competitive.

During my four years on the NCC football team, there were several outstanding players and some who went on to greater heights and positions of prominence after graduation. Some of those players were Butler "Blue Juice" Taylor, halfback and my former roommate; Welmon Britt, fullback; Otto Fuller, defensive back; Othan Fisher, tackle and who went on to play professionally in the Canadian Football League; and Ernest Warlick, end. Ernest went on to play professionally with Calgary of the Canadian Football League and later with the Buffalo Bills of the National Foot League.

Melvin Spencer, fullback, obtained his PhD and became a principal in the Washington, DC Public School System. Joseph Battle, quarterback, also obtained a PhD and taught mathematics at Duke University. Winifred Tillery, end, played professionally with the Philadelphia Eagles and Green Bay Packers but also received a PhD and became an assistant commissioner of education for the state of New Jersey and the superintendent of schools for Camden County, New Jersey. Amos Thornton, halfback, became a supervisor in the Recreation Department in Washington, DC. Jerome Evans, linebacker and halfback, became the first black coach at a predominantly white high school in Burlington, NC, and led his team to a state championship. Robert "R.O." Mason became the principal of a high school in Gastonia, North Carolina, that produced outstanding basketball stars, such as Eric "Sleepy" Floyd of Georgetown University and the NBA and James Worthy of the University of North Carolina and the NBA championship team of the Los Angeles Lakers. Vincent Reed played offensive tackle for West Virginia State College when North Carolina College played them in the Capital Classic in Washington, DC, in 1949, my freshman year in college. He later became the superintendent for the Public School System of the District of Columbia.

While matriculating at North Carolina College, I felt privileged and fortunate to have two outstanding teachers and coaches who made a significant impact on my teaching and coaching philosophy. Those individuals were John B. McLendon and Dr. Leroy Walker. Both individuals went on to receive national and international recognition. They were inducted into the hall of fame for their respective areas of expertise – Coach McLendon in the Basketball Hall of Fame in Springfield, Massachusetts, and Coach Walker (as I still address him) in the Track and Field Hall of Fame in Washington Heights, New York.

CAPS' STANDOUT—Harold Hunter, small as a basketball players go at 5 feet 10, is considered one of the best ball handlers in the American Basketball League. Hunter captained North Carolina College for four years. — (Photo Courtesy, THE WASHINGTON POST.

Courtesy of *The Washington Post*

Harold Hunter played basketball at North Carolina College and was the first African-American to sign an NBA contract to play for the Washington Capitols in 1950.

These five Eagle gridders were among football stars selected by Head Coach Herman Riddick for Awards Day honors.

Standing left is Charles Glenn, act tackle, who along with William Coward, right, standing received citation and letters. Coward was voted the player who contributed most to team's development.

Captain elect Ernest "Hands" Warlick, stellar flankman a versatile basketballer, is shov here center seated flanked Winifred Tillery, glue-finger end of last season and Rob Mason, right, Coach Riddic dependable tackle.

Courtesy Campus Echo
NCC Eagles in 1950

Courtesy *Miami Daily News*
Billy Coward (48) of North Carolina College chasing Oscar Norman (88) of Florida A&M out of bounds on the 2-yard line in the Orange Blossom Classic in 1951.

Shown here are the 30-odd members of the North Carolina College Eagles grid team of 1952.

Left to right, front row, are William Coward, Washington, D. C.; Maurice McNeil, Smithfield, N. C.; Melvin Spencer, Washington, D. C.; Winifred Tillery, Morehead City, N. C.; Robert Mason, Gastonia, N. C.; Joseph Battle, Rocky Mount, N. C.; Fred McNeil, Durham, N. C.; James Robinson, Charlotte, N. C.; Frederdick James, Kansas City, Mo.; and Jessie Allen, Durham, N. C.

Second row, left to right; Zeno Gaynor, Rocky Mount, N. C; Seabrew Ford, Chapel Hill, N. C.; Ardie Jenkins, Gary, Ind.; McCellan Matthews, Phoebus, Va.; Charles Staten, New Bern, N. C.; Linwood Johnson, Elizabeth City, N. C.; Charles Glenn, Winston-Salem, N. C. Thaddeus Beasley, Elizabeth City, N. C., and Horace Brown, Newport News, Va.

Third row, left to rights Floyd Jones, New Bern, N. C.; John Cameron, Durham, N. C.; Joseph Allen, Durham, N. C., Claude Mayfield, Suffolk, Va., Lawrence Pettis, Charlotte, N. C.; Charles Floyd, Wilson, N. C. Thomas Caldwell, Charlotte, N. C.; Jerome Evans, Goldsboro, N. C.; and Amos Thornton, Norfolk, Va.

Fourth row, left to right Oliver Boykin, trainer, Wilmington N. C.; Frank Wilson, Oxford, N C.; Ross Hines, Detroit, Mich, Edward Carroll, Oxford, N. C., Jack Aikens, Charlotte, N. C., Matthew Boone, Phoebus, Va., Carvis Bullock, Creedmoor, N. C.; Timothy Johnson, Kannapolis, N. C.; and Thomas Stith, Portsmouth, Va.

Stanback Photo
1952 North Carolina College Eagles

Chapter 4

I **FIRST MET** Coach McLendon as a youngster during the summer of 1939 while I was visiting my grandparents in Durham, North Carolina. My grandparents lived a block from the North Carolina College campus. Through the years in the 1940s when I visited them, I would often go into the gymnasium on campus to watch some of the pickup basketball games. Several years later I recalled how individuals representing the various colleges in the Colored Intercollegiate Athletic Association met to organize the first CIAA basketball tournament. The CIAA later became the Central Intercollegiate Athletic Association.

The first CIAA basketball tournament was held the last Thursday, Friday, and Saturday in February 1946 at Turner's Arena in Washington, DC. My brother, Leon, who was a freshman at NCC, came home that weekend to attend the tournament, and I tagged along with him. The NCC Eagles won the tournament in triple overtime against the Virginia Union Panthers. The final score was 64-56. My brother's fraternity brother Richard "Mice" Miller was one of the Mighty Mites or Whiz Kids, as they were called by their teammates. The way they played was certainly a testament to Coach McLendon's philosophy of strong defensive principles and fast-break basketball. Leroy Walker was the assistant coach.

After the football season of my freshman year, I played on the junior varsity basketball team, and Leroy Walker was our coach. I recall taking three classes from Coach McLendon. One of the classes was Kinesiology, the study of principles of mechanics and anatomy in relation to human movement. Coach McClendon told us he had attended the University of Kansas in

Lawrence, Kansas, and had taken classes from Dr. James Naismith, the inventor of the game of basketball, while there. The game was first played in Springfield, Massachusetts, where the Basketball Hall of Fame is currently located. I also recall Coach McLendon telling the class that one day, as a student at Kansas, he went swimming in the campus swimming pool. When he returned to go swimming the next day, he noticed the pool was being emptied. He asked an attendant what was wrong with the pool and was told the water was being emptied because he (McLendon) had been swimming in the pool. McLendon's response was, "Well, you may as well get used to emptying it regularly, because I am going to keep coming back." Unfortunately, the pool was being drained because Mclendon, an African-American, was using it.

In 1950 the CIAA basketball tournament was switched to Uline Arena, located at 3rd and M streets, Northeast, in Washington, DC. North Carolina College and West Virginia State played in the finals. I witnessed my alma mater, NCC, defeat West Virginia State 74-70 in a very exciting game. Harold Hunter was the co-captain of the champion NCC Eagles team. Other team members were Bill Young, Earl "Abdul" Davis, Tom Overton, co-captain Troy Weaver, Leo Rogers, George Green, Harry "Trees" Taylor, Ernie Warlick, and Jay Peterson.

This game also had a historical significance because Harold Hunter, who played for NCC, and Earl Lloyd, who played for WVS, would be the *first* African-American players to sign a contract to play in the NBA.

The basketball coach and other officials of the then-Washington Capitols staff were present and scouted the game. Later, after the game was over, Harold Hunter and Earl Lloyd received offers for a tryout with the Capitols. Coach McLendon and his assistant, Coach Walker, took Harold and Earl to the tryout, where they performed well. Afterward, according to Coach McLendon, Harold Hunter was the first of the two to sign a contract to play with the Capitols and became the first African-American player to sign with the NBA. Earl Lloyd signed immediately after Hunter.

Although Hunter was the first to sign, Earl Lloyd became the first African-American to play basketball in the NBA with the Washington Capitols. He later played with the Syracuse Nationals and Detroit Pistons. He also became the first African-American assistant coach in the NBA with the Detroit Pistons.

Harold Hunter was soon released and played basketball in the Eastern Basketball League. They had broken the color barrier, but Lloyd stated after Hunter's release that he didn't think the Washington Capitols owner would keep two African-American players. Hunter eventually started teaching and coaching in Wilmington, North Carolina. One of the players he coached was Meadowlark Lemon, who later became the "clown prince of basketball" when he played for the world-famous Harlem Globetrotters.

During my sophomore year at NCC, Charles "Tex" Harrison became a member of the basketball team. He was recruited from a high school in Houston, Texas. The next year, Sam Jones who played for Laurinburg Prep in Laurinburg, North Carolina, joined the team. Tex Harrison also went on to become a member of the Harlem Globetrotters and traveled around the world many times with the team. After his playing days were over, Tex became one of the coaches for the Globetrotters. Sam Jones left school for a tour of duty in the Army but returned to NCC after his discharge, where he played out his final years of eligibility. Jones was drafted by the Boston Celtics and played his entire professional career with the franchise. He was known around the NBA for his bank shot off the backboard or glass. He wore jersey number 24, which was retired by the Celtics at the end of his professional career. He was voted as one of the fifty best players in the history of the NBA. After Sam's playing days were over, he became the athletic director and basketball coach at Federal City College (FCC), now the University of the District of Columbia (UDC).

In the meantime, Coach McLendon left North Carolina College because there was a de-emphasis on athletics by the NCC administration. He took a job at Hampton Institute for a two-year period and then moved on to Tennessee State, where he led the Tennessee State Tigers to three National Association of Intercollegiate Athletics (NAIA) Basketball Championships in 1957, 1958, and 1959. While at Tennessee State he brought in two of his former players to assist him in coaching. One was Richard "Mice" Miller from his first CIAA tournament championship game in 1946; the other was Harold Hunter from the 1950 CIAA tournament championship game. Coach McLendon later left Tennessee State to coach at Kentucky State and then at Cleveland State and became the first African-American basketball coach with the Cleveland Pipers. He also conducted basketball clinics throughout the United States, several European countries, and Russia. He toured with several outstanding former collegiate players, including John Thompson, the former Providence College and Boston Celtic player and Georgetown University coach.

Coach Walker became famous in his own right. He was an assistant coach with the North Carolina College football team when my brother played on the team. Coach Walker coached the defensive line and was very good at it, according to my brother. As previously stated, he was also the assistant basketball coach. While assuming these positions, he was also the head track and field coach.

Some of his outstanding trackmen were Donald Leak, who became his first national champion in the hurdles. Leak later became the athletic director for the Gary School System in his hometown of Gary, Indiana. Lee Calhoun became Coach Walker's next shining star. Lee's name became popular as he won the 110-yard high hurdles in the 1956 and 1960 Olympics. Later on he became the track coach at Yale University and then at Western Illinois. Charles Foster was another outstanding hurdler at NCC. After graduation he became assistant track coach at the University of North Carolina in Chapel Hill.

Years later Coach Walker was invited by the State Department to coach and do consulting work in Africa and Israel. He became chancellor of North Carolina Central University (formerly known as North Carolina College) and president of the United States Olympic Committee in 1996, when the Olympics were held in Atlanta, Georgia.

I also took three classes from Coach Walker, one of which was Adaptive Physical Education. In the course we had to prescribe exercises for physically handicapped individuals. Years later I remembered many of the things I had learned in that course and applied them in real-life situations.

Chapter 5

AFTER GRADUATION FROM NCC on June 2, 1953, I returned home and began job hunting. I was fortunate enough to have been hired as a lifeguard and water-safety instructor at Francis Swimming Pool located at 25th and N streets, Northwest, in the Georgetown section of Washington, DC. This was not my long-term career goal, but the training I received at NCC served me well. During my senior year I had taken a class to become a lifeguard. In the lifesaving class I learned personal safety, elementary forms of rescue, swimming rescue, and resuscitation. Following that class, I took a class in water safety, which enabled me to become a water-safety instructor. All of the participants had to demonstrate at a high rate of proficiency all of the various strokes and kicks in swimming. We then had to teach a class in the fundamentals of swimming and how to practice and learn at the various stages of swimming (beginner, intermediate, and advanced). Because of this, I felt at ease and confident on my first day as a lifeguard and water-safety instructor.

That year, 1953, was the first year of integration in the swimming pools in Washington. A lot of the clientele who frequented Francis Swimming Pool came from the Dupont Circle, Georgetown, Foggy Bottom, and Embassy Row areas located along Massachusetts Avenue, Northwest. There was a very diverse group of people from all over the world – quite an international atmosphere.

There were three lifeguards assigned to Francis Pool, and all of us had our water-safety instructor's certificates. The other two lifeguards were Billy Williams and Albert Smith. Coincidentally, all of us had connections with NCC. Billy Williams, who was the oldest of the three of us, had played basketball in the mid-1940s for Coach McLendon; Albert "Needlehead" Smith, who had been two years ahead of me at NCC, was also a Kappa Alpha Psi fraternity brother of mine. We had also played on the Kappa intramural basketball championship team in 1951.

Swimming lessons for children were offered from 9:00 until 10:00 A.M. Monday through Friday, followed by a free swimming period from 10:00 until 11:30 A.M., during which they could swim on their own under the watchful eyes of the lifeguards. The pool was closed from 11:30 A.M. until 1:00 P.M., when it reopened to the general public, and remained open until 6:00 P.M. On Saturdays and Sundays the pool was generally very crowded and even more so if the weather was unusually warm. The pool capacity was 350 people, but I'm certain we were overcapacity on several weekends. Many of those who frequented the pool on weekends came to sunbath on the deck to see and be seen.

With only three lifeguards patrolling the pool area, I thought we did an outstanding job. We managed to keep the crowd under control and did not have any fatalities, although I will admit I had to make many rescues that summer. The first rescue of the summer was the most difficult I have ever experienced. I was sitting in the lifeguard's chair near a diving board at the deep end of the pool, which at that point was about nine to eleven feet deep, when a young boy about twelve years old ran out of the shower area, jumped onto the diving board, and dove into the water. He began to kick and stroke but didn't appear to be going anywhere nor did he seem to be able to breathe properly. After observing him for a short period of time I dove into the pool after him. When I got to him, he was face down in a horizontal position with his head turned away from me. Both of his arms and legs were in continual motion. None of the training I had received in the lifesaving courses taught me how to approach a drowning victim in that position, so I had to improvise quickly. I immediately went underwater, grabbed him by one of his legs, pulled him down, immediately went into a cross-chest carry, and resurfaced. As we reached the surface, he was struggling violently because he was having difficulty breathing. His arms and legs continued to swing and kick as I carried him to the pool deck. After I placed him on the deck, he was able to catch his breath and eventually began to breathe normally...and so did I.

I remember many of the individuals who frequented Francis Swimming Pool – some of them were really characters. One of them who stood out was Billy Stewart, a singer and musician. He was famous for his rendition of the song "Once I had a Secret Love." He was a heavyset man, and whenever he got on the diving board he drew attention. Frequently, he did a cannonball in which he would run off the diving board, landing in the water in a tucked position. As soon as he hit the water, there was a tremendously loud thud and water splashed all over the pool and nearby pool deck.

Another individual who frequented the pool, mostly on weekends when the pool was crowded, was quite the comedian. His name was Waldo "Petey" Green. He should not have been permitted to enter the pool area because he usually had been drinking. Petey, with his loud, raspy voice, got the attention of people in and around the pool as he talked and joked with his friends. He told one joke after the other, and soon the laughter became infectious and everyone was involved. It got to be a weekend affair because the swimmers recognized him when he showed up and were attentive whenever they heard his familiar, raspy voice.

Near the end of the swimming season that year, I was on duty in the lifeguard's chair near the entrance to the pool when I noticed Petey in the deepest part of the pool. He appeared to be rather passive but submerged underwater for a short period of time and then resurfaced. Again he submerged, but for a longer period of time, before he resurfaced the second time. I watched as he submerged for a third time but did not resurface within a reasonable length of time, so I jumped in and pulled him out of the water to safety. Petey left the pool that day soon after he regained his composure.

A year or so later Petey was incarcerated for a period of time, but after his release he became a community activist, and with his gift of gab, he was able to land a position as a talk show host on a local radio station. Members of the listening audience called in for his advice or his thoughts on a particular subject. He prefaced his statement to each caller by saying, "Talk to me." In 1968 when Martin Luther King was assassinated, people in the Washington, DC area began to riot. A lot of looting and burning took place in and around the U Street corridor and H Street, Northeast. Petey was asked to plead with the people over the radio to stop the looting and burning of property. His pleading seemed to have some effect.

Several years later, Petey was the guest speaker at a girls' sports award banquet. The Burdick girls served as cheerleaders for the Bell Vocational School's boys' athletic teams, where I was employed at the time as the coach of the basketball team. Because of my position, I had been invited to the banquet. Prior to the start of the banquet Petey approached me and said, "Thanks, Billy. I remember what you did for me years ago, and I would not be here today if you had not pulled me out of the pool." Around 2007 a movie was made about

Petey's life and his rise to a status of celebrity. Don Cheadle played the role as Petey in the movie, *Talk to Me*.

The swimming pool closed on Labor Day, September 1953. Two days later I got married, and a month later I was inducted into the United States Army. I was assigned to Fort Jackson, South Carolina, just outside Columbia, South Carolina, where I received my basic training. After basic training I was assigned to the Southeastern Signal School at Camp Gordon, Georgia. There I attended the high-speed radio operator school for six months. In the interim, my company commander asked me to conduct physical training for the company on a daily basis. He had apparently reviewed my record, noticed I majored in physical education in college, and decided I was sufficiently qualified to conduct those sessions. I also played basketball on one of the post's basketball teams.

After high speed radio operator school, I was assigned to the 7503rd Signal Company at Fort Buchanan, Puerto Rico. Shortly after I arrived there in the fall of 1954, I made a concerted effort to look for an apartment off base in anticipation of the arrival of my wife, Tamara, and our infant daughter, Terry, from Washington. I was able to find a one-bedroom apartment in Santuce, in the metropolitan area of San Juan. It was small and sparsely furnished but clean. There were other young military families who lived in the Rodriguez Moreno apartment building complex located at 1804 Fernando Juncos Avenue near Publico Stop 25 ½. On the day my family arrived, the first sergeant in my company was nice enough to get a Jeep and accompany me when I went to pick them up from the airport. I missed them terribly and was relieved to know that after months of being apart, we would be together again, although we did not know at the time if it would be for a few months or a year. Because I was living off base now, I knew my daily schedule would have to change; I would have to get up much earlier than before to be on the base in uniform for roll call at 6:00 A.M. But it was worth the sacrifice. We enjoyed exploring our new environment together.

One Sunday when I was off duty, I took them to the Army-Navy beach located near the Caribe Hilton and Normandy hotels in San Juan. It was a very warm day and an opportunity to relax and enjoy playing with Terry in the water. At one point I looked out and saw some rocks protruding from the water. They were about seventy-five yards away and had been placed there as a barrier to keep sharks and barracudas away from the swimming area. I told Tamara I was going to swim out to the rocks and back. She appeared to be somewhat apprehensive and pleaded with me not to swim out there. She said she was afraid something might happen. I reminded her of my lifeguard and water-safety instructor's certification and assured her that I would be all right. She watched as I began to swim slowly toward the rocks. When I reached the rocks, I turned to look back toward the shore and stepped down on something very sharp. I felt tremendous pain in my feet and reached out to balance myself against the rocks and immediately felt shearing pain in my hands as well. With each step the pain became more excruciating. I turned around and began swimming back to the beach. At the edge of the water I tried walking, but with each step the pain became more intense. I told my wife what had happened, and she immediately said, "You see? You should have listened to me." We gathered our belongings and immediately went to the Post dispensary at Fort Buchanan to see a doctor. I was told that I had stepped on sea urchins. The sea urchins had disintegrated under my skin like dirt and couldn't be removed. It was like having thirty or more splinters in your hands and feet. The doctor game me a tetanus shot and told me they would disappear over a period of time. They did but I will never forget that experience for as long as I live.

It was early fall and the baseball season had begun. This time of year the football season is in full swing in the States, but it is baseball season in Puerto Rico. Shortly after my arrival my company held tryouts for the company baseball team. I tried out for first base and was successful in winning the starting first baseman position. We played each of the other companies' teams twice, and before we realized it the company competition was over. My company's team ended up with a record of 4 wins and 4 losses.

Tryouts for the Fort Buchanan Post team were held after the company competitions were completed. Individuals from all the companies tried out. Several of the ballplayers had played for the farm teams in the Major Leagues, meaning they had been exposed to some pretty good coaching and had the potential to play in the Major Leagues one day. The competition was rather tough. However, I succeeded in making the final roster and played first base.

We played other military-post baseball teams on the island on a home-and-away schedule. The other teams were Camp Losey, Fort Brook, Henry Barracks, Ramey Air Force Base, and San Juan Navy Base. When we played away games it gave me an opportunity to see other parts of the island. Puerto Rico is sixty-five miles long and thirty-five miles wide and has a very picturesque mountain range and beautiful beaches.

At Fort Buchanan, our baseball field was a part of a golf course on the post. If you hit the baseball a long distance away, it might interfere with golfers on the green. On one of our scheduled games, Fort Buchanan was host team to Camp Losey. We knew that Camp Losey had the best military baseball team on the island; they also had several players who had played on the farm team of several Major League teams. Their starting pitcher was one of those players. Fortunately for me I had a very good game that particular day. The first time I came up to bat, I hit a double. The second time, I put down a bunt and beat it out for a single. In the bottom of the ninth inning with the score 3-1 in favor of Camp Losey, I came up with men on first and third bases and two outs. The pitcher started motioning for his infielders and outfielders to come in closer because he thought I wasn't going to hit the baseball very far. When he motioned for his teammates to come in, I motioned for them to move back, way back. When the pitcher was comfortable with the positions of his teammates, he began pitching to me. I hit the first pitch deep over the left-fielder's head for a triple, and both of the base runners scored – tying the score at 3-all. When the next batter came up to bat, I tried to distract the pitcher by taking long leads off of third base as if I were going to steal home. After the pitcher threw to the catcher for the third time, I ran a long way down the third baseline as if I were going to steal home. Instead, I turned around hurriedly and scampered back to third base. In the process I had caused the pitcher to hurry his delivery toward home plate and throw a wild pitch beyond the catcher. Had I continued to home plate, I would have scored the game-winning run. The pitcher finally struck out the batter, ending the inning. In the next inning, Camp Losey scored a run to take a one-run lead. When we had our turn at bat the pitcher retired the batters one, two, three, and Camp Losey won the game 4-3. To this day, I am certain that had I continued running toward home plate, I would have stolen home and Fort Buchanan would have won the game. After the game, one of the warrant officers who came to all of the games came up to me and said with a grin, "You did a Babe Ruth when you motioned for the players on Camp Losey's team to get back. Didn't you?"

I had been trying to make an adjustment in my batting by just meeting the ball after it had been pitched to me or just swinging to make contact with the ball. Fortunately, I was able to make this adjustment and managed to finish the season with a .384 batting average and led the team in home runs. When I was in high school I was a good fielder but couldn't hit my weight – which was 165 pounds.

The Puerto Rican professional baseball teams were active at this time. There was a league of six teams representing Caguas, Mayaguez, Ponce, Rio Piedras, San Juan, and Santurce. Several of the teams had individuals who played in the Major Leagues in the States. These players decided to hone their baseball skills and make some extra money by playing in Puerto Rico after the baseball season ended in the States. Some of those individuals were Don Zimmer, Steve Bilko, Elston Howard, Bob Thurman, and native Puerto Ricans, Orlando Cepeda, Roberto Clemente, and Luis "Canena" Marquez. Both Bob Thurman and Luis Marquez played for the Homestead Grays when I was the Grays' batboy.

At the conclusion of the baseball season, each company on the post at Fort Buchanan was responsible for sponsoring a Little League baseball team. The teams were made up of boys nine to twelve years old who were children of soldiers in their respective companies. I was selected as the manager of my company's Little League team. We had tryouts for the youngsters to enable us to assess their skills and determine what position each individual would play. All of the individuals who came out for the team were kept on the team roster; no one was turned away. After the rosters were completed, each company team played the other companies' teams in the league twice.

At the completion of league play an all-star team was selected by the managers and coaches of each team, but they could not vote for anyone on their own team. After the selection process had been completed for the all-star team to represent Fort Buchanan, I was selected to be the manager of the team. Our playing schedule included games against each of the Little League baseball teams on the other military posts on the island.

Almost as soon as the baseball season ended, the softball season was upon us. The warrant officer who followed the Fort Buchanan Post baseball team was selected as the manager of the post softball team. He asked me to come out to play on the softball team. I was flattered by the invitation and thanked him, but I wanted to spend more time with my family and indicated this to him. He continued to try to persuade me to change my mind and assured me that if I joined the team, I would be the first baseman. Until that point, I had spent all of my off-duty hours with the company's and post's baseball team as well as the Little League company and post baseball teams and had spent very little time with my wife and young daughter. But the warrant officer would not take no as an answer. He went to my company commander, Captain Lindstrom, and told him that I had made the decision not to play softball because of family obligations. Captain Lindstrom called me to the orderly room sometime later and pretty much told me to go out for the post softball team. It may not have been an order but I did as my commanding officer told me. The softball games were always played in the evening hours. We played fast-pitch softball. The pitcher's mound is closer to home plate than in baseball, and the softball is larger than the baseball. The adjustment from baseball to softball was not as easy for me as I had hoped – I either struck out or found myself being an easy out for the opposing team. However, after the softball season was over I did receive a promotion in rank from my company commander, which meant an increase in pay and more money for my family.

When the softball season ended, all of the company commanders received orders to select one soldier in their respective companies to take a lifeguard class at the post swimming pool. And, you guessed it, my company commander selected me. Upon arriving at the pool, I met a soldier who was chosen to conduct the class. As we talked, he told me he had his senior lifeguard certificate but was not certified as a water-safety instructor. Because of this, he wasn't qualified to conduct the class. I let him know that I was a certified water-safety instructor, and he in turn told the officer in charge of the class. The officer approached me and asked where I had been certified to teach as a water-safety instructor. I told him I had received my certification in Washington, DC. He immediately contacted the American Red Cross in DC and asked for a confirmation of my qualifications. The confirmation was sent back to the officer, and I ended up conducting the lifeguard's class.

As before, it seemed that one season ran into the other. Basketball season was about to begin, and I was chosen to coach the company basketball team. We went through a brief schedule – as usual, playing the other companies' teams. Fortunately, we had a winning season. After we had completed the company competitions, tryouts for the post basketball team were held. After very competitive tryouts the Fort Buchanan basketball team was selected, and I was one of the fortunate ones to make the team. During the tryouts I hustled and played very aggressively, causing the ball handlers to throw erratic passes and make turnovers through intercepted passes. I made steals and rebounded on defense. I always prided myself on being in good physical condition and was able to run tirelessly. These were the reasons, in my opinion, that I was able to make the team.

As usual, we played each of the other military post teams twice on a home-and-away basis, comparable to the schedule we had in baseball. This was significant to me because I got another opportunity to travel and see the island again. I had taken Spanish in high school and college and utilized those skills when interacting with local personnel on the post and during my travels throughout the island. I had the opportunity to converse in Spanish regularly and enjoyed the chance to practice this new language. I had a large vocabulary but didn't feel confident in my ability to speak the language. I had to become accustomed to the Puerto Rican accents as well. Spanish is a language in which most of the words end in vowels and the words often sounded, to me, like they were running together. I tried to listen carefully as someone conversed with me in Spanish, but if the individual spoke with an accent, it was somewhat difficult to translate at first. However, being in an environment where Spanish was spoken daily, I eventually became accustomed to the accents. I remember one Puerto Rican asking me if I were from Spain because he thought I spoke Castilian Spanish. My high school Spanish teacher, Mr. D.A. Lanauze, was from Ponce, Puerto Rico. I had the privilege to travel to Ponce on a couple of occasions. On one occasion while there, I found out that Mr. Lanauze's brother played third base for the Ponce professional league baseball team.

I recall my college Spanish instructor, Professor Charles Holmes, telling the class, "You'll never know when you might need Spanish." Most of the class laughed, including myself. He repeated himself then said, "Don't laugh because you will never know when you might need Spanish." He went on to say he was telling another class the same thing a few years before and most of the students in that class also laughed. In that class was a student whose name was Harry "Trees" Taylor. He was a member of the North Carolina College Eagles 1950 CIAA Championship basketball team. After graduation he went on to play basketball for the world-famous Harlem Globetrotters, who toured and played in Central and South American countries. Trees wrote Professor Holmes a letter in which he indicated that he was among the students who laughed when he told them they never knew when they might need to know how to speak Spanish. Professor Holmes read the letter to my class and again repeated the statement. I smiled again and thought I would never need to know Spanish; I was only taking the class because a foreign language was required. How wrong I was and how grateful I was that I could use that language skill later in life.

There I was after graduation from college being inducted into the Army, with eight weeks of basic training at Fort Jackson, South Carolina, six months of high-speed radio operations school at Camp Gordon, Georgia, and then an assignment to the 7503rd Signal Corps Company at Fort Buchanan, Puerto Rico. I wrote a letter to Professor Holmes and told him I had laughed when he told my class that we will never know when we might need Spanish; and as destiny would have it, I ended up being stationed in

Puerto Rico for one full year and a month, where the native language is Spanish. I was later told that he read my letter to the Spanish classes he was teaching at the time.

B. Coward's Personal Collection
Billy Coward, first baseman for Fort Buchanan, Puerto Rico, 1954.

B. Coward's Personal Collection

Coach Billy Coward (standing on the left) with
Little League Company Baseball team,
Fort Buchanan, Puerto Rico, 1954.

B. Coward's Personal Collection
Fort Buchanan, Puerto Rico Basketball Team 1955, Billy Coward (55)

B. Coward's Personal Collection
Francis Swimming Pool lifeguards, 1956, L-R: Victor Stone, Billy Williams, Albert Smith, Billy Coward.

B. Coward's Personal Collection
Francis Swimming Pool lifeguards, 1958
L-R: Oswell Sykes, Ronald Payne, Charles Dobson, Billy Coward

B. Coward's Personal Collection
Chuck Dobson watches as Billy Coward gives Mr. Bob Baker
(Francis Swimming Pool manager) a birthday gift from the lifeguards, 1958

B. Coward's Personal Collection
Billy Coward, lifeguard at Francis Swimming Pool, 1958

B. Coward's Personal Collection
Francis Swimming Pool, 1958, Billy Coward cross-chest carrying Lawrence Wolf

Chapter 6

AFTER SERVING A two-year tour of duty in the Army I received an Honorable Discharge in September of 1955 and soon afterward started working in the Main Post Office in Washington, DC, located at North Capitol and Massachusetts Avenue, Northeast. While working in the post office, I organized and coached the post office basketball team. The team was comprised of mostly T-men, post office employees who worked halftime, usually four hours an evening, and for the most part had played basketball in high school. Most of them were going to college during the day and working at night.

The post office basketball team played its games in the DC Recreation League at Roosevelt High School's gymnasium, located at 13th and Upshur streets, Northwest. There were six teams in the league, and we played each of the other teams twice. The games were scheduled on Wednesdays at 7:00, 8:00, and 9:00 P.M. At the conclusion of league play, the post office team ended up in second place in league standings.

If I thought my life as a lifeguard and water-safety instructor had ended prior to my life as a soldier, I was mistaken. While still working as a postal employee, I found myself working at Francis Swimming Pool again in the summer of 1956, perhaps as much out of necessity as desire, because my young family was increasing. During that time, the swimming pools in Washington were run and operated by Government Services, Inc. The water-safety instructors were paid by the DC Recreation Department for teaching swimming classes to the youth in the city during the morning sessions. During the afternoon and early evening hours, Government Services, Inc. paid for the operation of the pools, including the salaries of the staff.

The instructional program for young swimmers at most of the pools consisted of several teaching stations: one for the basic fundamentals of swimming for the beginner; another for the advanced beginner; a third for the intermediate swimmer; and another for the advanced swimmer. When the group instructional sessions ended, each student had an opportunity to practice the skills learned in their classes under the watchful eye of a certified lifeguard. As my children grew older they also took advantage of the opportunity to participate in this wonderful instructional swimming program for the city's youth. They not only learned to swim but enhanced their skills and became lifeguards themselves as teenagers.

Francis Swimming Pool is located near Georgetown not far from Embassy Row along Massachusetts Avenue. Many of the individuals in the swimming classes were children of ambassadors from other countries or children of embassy employees, in one capacity or another. Because of the proximity of the pool to the embassies and the use of the pool by individuals from the embassies, I had the opportunity to teach children from many foreign countries to swim, and in return they taught me some of their languages and customs of their native lands. This interaction with them helped me to understand that people are different at the same time and the same at different times. We are different in the way we look and talk, in our customs, mores, and beliefs, in our choice of religions, and the way we practice our faiths. But I believe that we are the same when it comes to the basic needs cited in Maslow's Hierarchy of Needs: biological, safety, social, self-esteem, and self-actualization. According to Maslow's theory, we must first achieve one before we can move on to the next. My education continues with each experience and opportunity to exchange ideas and information with others.

Once a week the lifeguards and water-safety instructors worked with physically or mentally impaired individuals. It was a revelation to work with and assist them in learning to swim or even to relax in the pool. In greeting or speaking to them each day, I asked how they were doing. Their reply was always, in spite of their disabilities, fine, good, or something positive. Yet we come in contact with individuals who have all of their mental and physical capacities but who complain frequently about how they feel or the problems they have encountered. We should learn from those who are less fortunate than we.

Prior to taking positions as lifeguards, those of us who were assigned to the public swimming pools throughout the city had to take the lifeguard's test every year. The Red Cross had the responsibility to administer the test, and the representative responsible for administering the test was Joe Aronoff. He was a no-nonsense individual who put us through a very rigorous routine. We had to demonstrate a very high level of efficiency before we could become certified to continue our jobs at the swimming pools. Because of the difficulty of the tests, we also had to be in very good physical condition in order to pass. We were taught that circumstances could arise at the pools that may become life-or-death situations requiring alertness, split-second decisions, and physical readiness.

Joe Aronoff was a big man who weighed around 240 pounds. I remember so vividly how I had to swim twenty-five yards across the pool to get a potential drowning victim – that "victim" happened to be Joe. As I made my approach and my reverse move and got within three yards of Joe, he lunged at me and grabbed me with a front headlock and held me tightly. I immediately submerged to the bottom of the pool with Joe still holding me. After staying submerged for a short period of time and knowing a drowning victim would want to get to the surface to breathe, I went into a front head-hold release, leveled him off into a cross-chest carry, and pushed off from the bottom at an angle enabling me to carry him in a horizontal position until we reached the pool deck. He was quite a load.

Joe's son, Marty Aronoff, is a statistician for the NFL and the Washington Redskins and also for the NBA and the Washington Wizards.

Throughout the summer months of the late 1950s and 1960s, I served as a lifeguard, water-safety instructor, and swimming-team coach at Francis Swimming Pool. I taught my daughters, Terry, Donna, and Vicki to swim at very young ages. I recall how difficult it was to get Donna, our middle daughter, to put her head underwater and open her eyes while her head was submerged. One day as I taught the other children in my class the beginning fundamentals of swimming, Donna observed from the deck. About a week later during the free-swim period, Donna came up to me and said, "Dad, I can open my eyes underwater now." She led me to the baby pool and put her head underwater. As she did this, I put my hand underwater and held out a certain number of fingers and asked her to tell me how many. When she accurately responded I knew she had reached a turning point. From that moment on she took off learning the basic fundamentals of swimming at a very rapid pace.

Before our youngest daughter, Vicki, was three years old, I worked with her individually on the basic fundamentals of swimming, first in shallow water and then in deep water. She started jumping off the low diving board and swimming to the ladder in eleven feet of water. After gaining enough confidence to jump off the low board, I encouraged her to jump off the high tower, fifteen feet above the pool deck. She started climbing the ladder to reach the top, but because her legs were so short at that age (two years and ten months) she could only take one step at a time. When she finally got to the top, I told her to do the same thing she had done when jumping off the low diving board. I assured her that I would be in the pool when she jumped to help just in case she needed me. Vicki hesitated a moment, looked down, and then jumped. After she hit the water, she began kicking and dog peddling. She opened her eyes, and I told her to keep kicking and swim to the pool deck. She did, and when she got out of the pool, without being prodded to do so, she immediately went back to the ladder to the high tower and began climbing again – one step at a time. She reached the top, walked out to the diving board, and jumped again. At that moment she had a captive audience. You could hear the spectators and other swimmers say, "Look at that little girl." Each subsequent time when she climbed to the tower, she stood for a moment to see if anyone was watching. When she knew she had an audience, she took the plunge.

As the summers passed, the members of the Francis swimming team participated in swimming meets against swim teams from the other public swimming pools throughout the city. Dual meets against other pools were held prior to the city-wide championship meet. Over a period of time the following pools sent individual representatives to the city-wide champion meet: Anacostia, Banneker, Douglas, Dunbar, East Potomac, Fort Dupont, Fort Stanton, Francis, McKinley, the Natatorium, Oxon Run, Randall, Rosedale, Takoma, and Upshur.

In 1953 the manager of Francis Swimming Pool was a middle-aged man from Washington, Pennsylvania, named Bob Baker. Mr. Baker, as everyone around the pool called him, was a kind and gentle man who had worked at Francis for years and loved sharing a bit of the history of the pool with the young upstarts who worked with him. He told me about Montague Cobb, who preceded him as manager while continuing to pursue his education. Montague Cobb was a native Washingtonian and a graduate of my alma mater, Dunbar High School. In the ensuing years, he received an MD degree from Howard University and became Dr. Cobb, Chairman of the Department of Anatomy at Howard.

He also told me about Charles Drew and his brother, Joe Drew, who were lifeguards at Francis in previous years. They were also native Washingtonians who were very much involved in athletics and coaching. Dr. Drew was also a graduate of my alma mater, Dunbar High School, and became a four-letterman. He continued to play football as an undergraduate at Amherst College and after graduation coached at Morgan State College before enrolling in medical school and receiving his MD degree. He is credited with the development of the blood bank and is known as the first to introduce a system for storing blood plasma. His brother, Joe Drew, taught at Terrell Junior High School and Cardozo High School and served in an administrative capacity at Garnet Patterson Junior High School in Washington, DC. He also officiated at high school football and basketball games in the area.

In the 1940s and 1950s there were many individuals in this area who represented their high school swim teams and received swimming scholarships to attend college, or they joined swim teams after tryouts at the college or university in which they were enrolled. During the summer months, many of these individuals returned home and became lifeguards or water-safety instructors. Among those individuals was Stanley Gainor, a graduate of Armstrong who attended Tennessee State. Stanley later taught and coached the swim team at Cardozo. Clarence "Penny" Pendelton graduated from Dunbar High School and then enrolled in Howard University. Penny later became the swim team coach at Howard and in later years was appointed Chairman of the US Commission on Civil Rights by President Ronald Reagan in 1983. Elmer Bowman graduated from Dunbar before entering West Virginia State. He pursued a degree in dentistry, following in his father's footsteps, and has worked in that capacity for a number of years in his native city, Washington, DC. Dr. Bowman's older brother, James "Jimmy" Bowman, became a physician specializing in hematology. He is the father of Valerie Jarrett, one of the senior advisors to President Barack Obama. Charles "Chuck" Dobson attended Dunbar then enrolled in Tennessee State. Chuck was a jet pilot in the US Air Force and held the rank of lieutenant colonel. Ronald Payne is also a Dunbar graduate and a graduate of Tennessee State; however, he and Chuck matriculated at both schools at different times. Thomas "Tommy" Jeter, another Dunbar alum, pursued his undergraduate degree at Howard University before enrolling in Howard's School of Dentistry. Dr. Jeter has become an outstanding instructor on the faculty there. Joseph "Joe" Drew, Jr., whose father and uncle have been mentioned earlier in this book, is another Dunbar and Howard University graduate who was also another exceptional swimmer. He was also a jet pilot in the Air Force with the rank of lieutenant colonel. James "Jimmy" Featherstone graduated from Dunbar and is another

Dunbar graduate who also attended Tennessee State. All of the individuals mentioned above have made significant contributions to the field and sport of swimming as high school and college students and even beyond.

During the late 1950s Spingarn High School's basketball team was coached by Dr. William Roundtree. He had previously been a teacher at Dunbar High School and the coach of the junior varsity basketball team when I was a student there in the late 1940s. Dr. Roundtree invited some of the basketball players whom he had known when he was at Dunbar to come to Spingarn during one of the Christmas holidays to scrimmage against his team. He wanted to give his young high school players the experience of playing against older and more experienced players. I recall that Donald Lipscomb, Kermit Banks, Melvin Jones, Ollie Thompson, and I were among the players from Dunbar's basketball team who participated in those scrimmages.

At Spingarn Dr. Roundtree produced some outstanding basketball teams. Some of his players were Garland "Chin" Logan; Roy "Monk" Wilkins; Donald Hicks, who became a very good tennis player in later years; and Ollie Johnson, who attended the University of San Francisco and was drafted by and played professionally for the Boston Celtics. Others included Dave Bing, who played for Syracuse University as an undergraduate and then professionally for the NBA Detroit Pistons and the Washington Bullets (now the Washington Wizards). After retirement from the NBA, Dave became the founder and owner of an automobile supply firm in Detroit. He later became mayor of Detroit.

After his coaching days were over, Dr. Roundtree became principal of Calvin Coolidge High School in Northwest Washington. He soon left the DCPS system to become an administrator in the physical education department at Howard University.

In 1958 I joined the DC Collegians football team. The Collegians were members of the District of Columbia Amateur Football Conference. Other Athletic Club teams in the conference were the Cavaliers, Anacostia, the Stonewalls, and Saint Cyprian. The games were scheduled and played in Murkirk, MD, Brandywine, MD, and Banneker Stadium at Georgia Avenue and Barry Place in Washington.

The Collegians team was compromised of players who had played football in college, for the most part. The team was coached by Adam Scott, who had played at Central State, and Arthur Smith, who had played at Howard

University – both were considered to be football greats. Some of the players on the team were Curtis Moore, Eugene Smith, Ernest "Bum" Thompson, Ulysses Barton, Paul Woodard, Francis "Jackie" Queen, Milton "Lucky" Jordan, Mathew Boone, Amos Thornton, Sidney "Nip" Parker, Herman "Stump" Baylor, Robert "Bob" Johnson, and Milton "Skeeter" Douglas. Our games were usually played on weekends, and because I was able to practice only once a week, I usually kicked off, occasionally punted, and played defensive back.

Some of the games were memorable. I recall one game in which the Collegians were playing the Stonewalls in Murkirk, MD. It was a close but exciting game that we were fortunate to win. However, I remember at one point during the game the Stonewalls were deep in their own territory on a fourth down and were forced to punt from their end zone. Reggie Lee was sent in to punt. He punted the ball, a nice high spiraling kick that went seventy yards in the air, came down, and rolled an additional thirty yards to our end zone, where the Stonewalls downed the ball. I thought it was one of the best punts I had ever seen either in high school, college, or the pros. Later on in the game, Reggie got hurt and his jaw was broken. In those days we didn't wear face masks on our helmets. After the game was over Reggie told me he was going to the hospital to have his jaw wired before going to Mexico to play winter league baseball. Reggie was a three-sport athlete at Armstrong and a standout in all three sports.

In September of 1960 I began teaching and coaching at my alma mater, Garnet Patterson Junior High School. It was truly a pleasure for me to return to the school where I first became exposed to organized sports. At Garnet Patterson I taught fundamentals of several popular sports in my gym classes – football, basketball, baseball, and track. It was quite rewarding to me to realize the contribution that I was making to the athletic development of another generation of young men. My students had an opportunity to demonstrate the skills they had learned in class by participating in intramural football against teams on the same grade level. Some of those individuals who participated and went on to play football in high school were Cole McLlwain, Allen McDuffie, Larry Featherstone, John Bossard, Michael Jones, and Benjamin Wrenn. Each of these players went to Bell Vocational High School, which was a powerhouse at that time. Each of them played a significant role in the Inter-High championship teams of 1964, 1965, and 1966.

Michael Jones was the starting quarterback on the 1964 championship team. Benjamin Wrenn was the starting quarterback on the 1965 and 1966 teams. Wrenn also made the All-Metropolitan High School Football Team. Charles Stovall enrolled in Cardozo and developed into a very good offensive lineman. As a result, Stovall made the All-High Football Team. Because of his athletic prowess, Brig Owens, the former Redskins outstanding defensive back, assisted Stovall in getting a football scholarship to Cincinnati University, Brig's alma mater. Richard Fleming also played football and ran track at Cardozo. He ultimately became a captain in the Washington, DC Fire Department.

Garnet Patterson fielded a basketball team to play other junior high school teams in the DC Public Schools – Francis, Shaw, Banneker, MacFarland, Deal, Randall, Backus, and Langley. Games were played on a home-and-home basis. We were fortunate to win most of the games played during the 1961-62 and 1962-63 basketball seasons. Some of the Garnet Patterson players who graduated and later participated in varsity basketball on the high-school level at Bell Vocational were Kirby Burks, Allan "Huckle Buck" Hill, John Bossard, Larry Featherstone, Luke Williams, and Benjamin Wrenn.

Harold Monroe attended McKinley and later became a pharmacist. Lamar McCoy went to Western and made *The Washington Post*'s All-Metropolitan High School Team. He also received a basketball scholarship to attend Southwestern Missouri State University. Wayne Fleshman continued his varsity career at Dunbar.

The Athletic Department for the DC Public Schools sponsored two track meets for the junior high schools – one for all the schools in the east, which would include all of the schools located in the Northeast and Southeast sections of Washington; the other for all of the schools located in the Northwest and Southwest sections of the city. Because Garnet Patterson was located in the Northwest section of the city, we participated in the Western Division against Randall, Jefferson, Shaw, Francis, Gordon, Deal, MacFarland, and Paul junior high schools. In 1961 Garnet Patterson was represented by several individuals who were medal winners. At the Western Division track meet, Michael Gage won the 100-yard dash; Freddy Long won the shot put; Allen Burriss won the broad jump; Sterling Ross, Donald Carver, Calvin Webster, and Clarence Webster won relays.

Throughout my teaching and coaching I always encouraged any of the students interested in playing sports to go out for track because participating in track would help enhance their overall conditioning, coordination, stamina, flexibility, and endurance. To increase speed and quickness, they were encouraged to run up hills. Coaches at the next level are always looking for individuals who can demonstrate these characteristics in the sports they coach.

After the 1963 basketball team's regular season schedule was over, I arranged to have the school team play the teachers. The teachers' team included Harry Burke, a former trackman at Hampton Institute and later director of graphic arts for the DC Public Schools; Carter Bowman; Edward Armstead, who later became principal at Paul Junior High School; Napoleon "Nappy" Lewis, a former teammate of Clarence "Big House" Gaines, who played at Morgan State in the early 1940s on one of their outstanding football teams. Nappy Lewis later became the principal of H.D. Woodson Senior High School and subsequently an assistant superintendent for the DC Public Schools. Billy Hunter, the former Washington Redskins defensive back, served as a substitute teacher while he attended law school at Howard University. After Billy Hunter got his law degree, he moved out to California and became the mayor of Oakland. After his term as mayor of Oakland ended, he became the executive director of the National Basketball Players Association. I was also on the 1963 teachers' team.

The game was played before a packed house of students and teachers in Garnet Patterson's small gymnasium. It was all in fun, but as hard as the students played, they did not outdo the teachers. However, I have to admit that the teachers only won by a very few points.

During the 1963-64 school year, Garnet Patterson received a new principal, and the new administration did not permit us to field any athletic teams. As a result, I offered my services to assist the basketball coach at Dunbar High School, Mr. Lois Williams, who happened to have been my former high school coach. Although Mr. Williams let me put the team through very rigorous practices, I was not coaching from the bench on the days of scheduled games. The team was successful in winning seventy percent of the games they played, a credit to Mr. Williams as well as the student athletes, of course.

Some of the players on that team were William "Bill" Otey; Clarence Monroe; Rudy Peterson, who became the basketball coach at H.D. Woodson High School years later; and Wendell Hart, who became the basketball coach at Phelps Vocational High School a few years later. There were also two managers for the basketball team, Eddie Davis and Johnny Grier, who went on to establish reputations for themselves in sports.

Eddie Davis was a former student at Garnet Patterson and played on the basketball team during his senior year at Dunbar. After graduation he matriculated at West Virginia State and continued to play basketball on the school's varsity basketball team. Eddie was a late bloomer but developed into a very good basketball player. He later became a very successful basketball coach at

Bowie State, a member of the CIAA. Eddie led the Lady Bulldogs to the CIAA Tournament Championship in 1997, 1998, and 1999. He was also selected as the outstanding coach for three consecutive years. Eddie moved on to Delaware State in the Mid-Eastern Athletic Conference (MEAC) to coach the Lady Hornets and lead them on to the MEAC tournament championship in 2007.

Johnny Grier went into the US Air Force for four years after graduating from Dunbar. He received his undergraduate and master's degrees from the University of the District of Columbia. He began refereeing high school basketball games; in fact, he refereed several basketball games I coached while I was at Bell Vocational High. He was a member of the Eastern Board of Officials. He also refereed football games in the MEAC and became a field judge in the NFL. He became the first African-American referee in the NFL in 1981. Additionally, he officiated in Super Bowl XXII between the Washington Redskins and the Denver Broncos in 1988.

I didn't miss too many DCPS Inter-High basketball games during that era and managed to see many of the games during the 1963-64 season. I particularly enjoyed watching the games in which Cardozo played because they were an exciting team. They were coached by Frank Bolden. There were two players on the team, Phillip "Bo" Scott and Aaron Webster, who were lightning fast and would have been terrific assets to a college team playing fast-break basketball, in my thinking. I mentioned to Frank Bolden that I thought the two of them would fit in well with the brand of ball that Tennessee State played. I offered to call Harold Hunter, who had succeeded John McLendon as head coach at Tennessee State, to see if he would consider offering scholarships to Phil and Aaron. Frank was delighted. He had coached Hillary Brown at Cardozo before Hillary finished high school. When Hillary graduated, he enrolled in Tennessee State on a basketball scholarship and played under Coach McLendon. I called Harold and gave him my assessment of these two young men. He listened carefully but did not make any immediate commitments, but he ultimately offered both of them scholarships to attend Tennessee State.

During the summer of 1964, the International Deaf Olympics for Track and Field was held at the University of Maryland College Park campus. Track and field athletes from all over the world participated in this event. The athletes were hearing and speech impaired. There were several teachers and coaches from the DCPS who volunteered to officiate at these meets. Among them were Alphonso "Bud" Liggins, who served as the starter for all of the running events; Frank Bolden, who was a judge at the finish line for the running events; and myself, who served as judge for the long jump in the field event.

I was truly amazed to see athletes from all walks of life perform at such a high rate of efficiency despite their limitations. In the running events, they had to keep their eyes on the starter's gun and watch the sight of the smoke from the gun as he pulled the trigger or feel the thud or vibration when the trigger was pulled to know when to start. As I watched the start of the many heats, I was quite surprised at how few false starts there were, given the fact that these athletes were challenged with speech or hearing impairments. One could sense an eerie silence throughout the stadium as the athletes performed.

I realized how fortunate I was to have all of my senses – the ability to see, smell, hear, touch, and speak. When the athletes and officials had a lunch break, they went to the University of Maryland cafeteria to eat, where there was a wide variety of foods and desserts to select from. In front of some of the food items were signs to indicate what the food was, but for others there were no signs at all. To those for whom English was not their native language, understanding the signs presented a problem. I noticed that many of the athletes did not recognize some of the food dishes, or perhaps they were not familiar with the way the food had been prepared. In these cases, they picked up the plates the food was displayed on then smelled the food in order to identify it. If it was a smell with which they were familiar, they placed it on their tray. If it was a smell they either did not recognize or like, they put it back. At the conclusion of all of the events, the athletes who came in first, second, or third in individual events were recognized for their accomplishments and given medals as they took their places on the winners' stand.

photo by L.A. Hasbrouck, Jr.
US Post Office Clerks 1958, L-R kneeling: Ron Taylor, Charlie Faulkner, Bob Stroud, Kenneth Tapscott, Tiny Grimes. L-R standing: Ellsworth Jenkins, Leroy Settles, Russell Grigsby, Joe Mitchel, Dudley Millen, Coach Billy Coward

photo by L. A. Hasbrouck, Jr.
New Cage Outfit Semi-Pro Basketball Team, 1959
L-R kneeling: Ollie Thompson, Russell Grigsby, Terry Hatchett, Gary Mays, Donald Lipscomb
L-R standing: Coach Billy Coward, Kenny Washington, Murdock Scofield, Mickey Buchanan, Rip Frazier

B. Coward's Personal Collection
Daughter Vicki Coward jumping off high board before she was 3 years old at Francis Swimming Pool, summer 1960

Davidson Photo
Garnet Patterson Track Team 1960-61
Standing L-R: Coach V. Harris, J. Robinson, M. Cage, L. Wigglesworth, J. Logan, F. Long, A. Doctor, J. Addison, J. Bell, N. Cooper, K. McKinney, L. Green, Coach B. Coward
Kneeling L-R: R. Wigglesworth, D. Carver, W. Reynolds, M. Cardwell, C. Corbett, E. Cook, C. Hamer, C. Webster, CA. Webster, M. Matthews, W. Wanzer, W. Jeffries, R. Williams

Davidson Photo
Garnet Patterson Track Team Medal Winners 1961
L-R: Coach B. Coward, M. Gage, F. Long, D. Carver, A. Burriss, S. Ross, Cl. Webster, Cal. Webster

Davidson Photo
Garnet Patterson Basketball Team 1961-62
Kneeling L-R: R. Williams, J. Burke, E. Robertson, M. Jones, L. Bryant, J. Stowe
Standing L-R: F. Long, J. Pierce, H. Monroe, L. Hill, L. McCoy, J. Latney, Coach B. Coward

Davidson Photo

Garnet Patterson Junior High Basketball Team 1962-63
Kneeling: Coach Billy Coward
Standing L-R: M. Howard, J. Burks, L. Bryant, G. Morgan, J. Pierce, L. Hill, L. Featherstone, W. Fleshman, L. McCoy, B. Wrenn, R. Harris, L. Williams, L. Stokes, L. Davis

Davidson Photo

Garnet Patterson Junior High School Basketball Team 1963-64
From L-R: Eddie Robinson, Ronald Melchor, John Bossard, L. Anderson, Benjamin Wren, Lamar McCoy, Wayne Fleshman, Larry Featherstone, Mgr. Allen McDuffie, Coach Billy Coward

B. Coward's Personal Collection
Garnet Patterson 1964 track team

Chapter 7

DURING THE 1964-65 school year, the principal at Garnet Patterson, Mrs. Margaret Labat, gave me permission to organize a school basketball team again. By not having a team the previous year, I had no holdovers to build the basketball team around. We played our first game away at Backus Junior High School without three of our better players. Backus had a young, eighth-grade center who could jump and rebound exceptionally well. We lost to Backus that day by a large margin. However, we had a return game against Backus on our home court, and we managed to win the game by one point with the three players who did not play in the starting lineup of the first game. The eighth-grade center on Backus' team was James Brown.

After junior high school, James Brown, or JB as he is known to many attended DeMatha Catholic High School and became an outstanding basketball player there. In 1969 he was an All-Metropolitan selection and *The Washington Post* Player-of-the-Year during his senior year at DeMatha. Along with Floyd Lewis, another All-Metropolitan basketball player from Western High School, he was recruited to play basketball at Harvard University. It may seem a bit unusual, but Senator Edward Kennedy placed a full-page advertisement in the sports section of *The Washington Post* to try to recruit both JB and Floyd to play at Harvard. This is where they eventually enrolled after being recruited by other colleges and universities.

After graduation from Harvard, Floyd attended law school and is now a practicing attorney. JB was a first-round pick in the NBA draft by the Atlanta Hawks in 1973. Unfortunately, he was the last player on the team to be cut by Coach Fitzsimmons. JB joined the Washington Bullets and played with the

Bullets in the Urban Coalition Summer League at Roosevelt High School. I saw several of those games that summer, and JB definitely was playing very well – much better, in my opinion, then some of the other players who were playing in the same position on the team. I said to him, "JB, you ought to make this team." He seemed somewhat surprised, responding, "You think so, Coach?" My answer was yes, but I did not know at the time if there were no-cut clauses in the contracts or what the circumstances may have been with the other players. He clearly outplayed some of the other players, but he did not make the team. However, he went on to find his niche in sports broadcasting in television. He has worked on national television at CBS, ABC, and Fox.

Some of my best junior high school players who played for Garnet Patterson against the Backus team that JB played on were Michael Jackson, Jake Jones, and Roosevelt James. The three of them continued their secondary education at Cardozo High School and played basketball under the very able tutelage of Coach Harold Dean. Michael Jackson made the High School All-Metropolitan Basketball Team his senior year and went on to play collegiate basketball at a junior college in California. After that, he played in Los Angeles at a four-year college. He ultimately joined the pros and played with the Virginia Squires in the American Basketball Association. Among his teammates were Julius "Doctor J" Erving and George "The Iceman" Gervin. Both of them left the ABA and became famous in the NBA. Doctor J played with the Philadelphia 76ers, and The Iceman played with the San Antonio Spurs. Jake Jones played college basketball at the District of Columbia Teachers College.

Roosevelt James later played with the DC recreational team the Kerlips, formed in 1964. A number of fellows in the area who had played basketball at one level or another as students got together to form the team which was named after two of the organizers, Kermit Banks and Donald Lipscomb. Thus, the team became known as the Kerlips. Kermit and Donald were two of my teammates at Dunbar during the 1948-49 basketball season. The Kerlips joined the Washington, DC Recreation League and played as a team in 1964, 1965, and 1966. League teams were established at different playing sites throughout each section of the city; our home site and league was at Roosevelt High School in Northwest DC. We played each team in that league once, and the team who finished in first place in the round robin received a trophy. That team was also invited to compete against other first-place teams from other recreational leagues throughout the city. The single elimination playoff to decide the DC Recreation Department's city champion was played at Ballou

Senior High School. We were fortunate to win the championship in the 1964 title game rather easily and won another trophy as well.

In the ensuing seasons we found ourselves in a similar position: We were able to finish in first place in the Roosevelt league and returned to Ballou to face other winners from other leagues throughout the city. In the finals for each of the last two years, we met up with a formidable team comprised of some talented basketball players. On that team were Sandy Freeman, an individual whom I played against in high school when he played at Phelps; Andrew Johnson, a lieutenant on the DC Police Force and the brother of Ollie Johnson, a Boston Celtics player; Marty Tapscott, a former Spingarn and Howard University basketball player who was a DC Police captain and would later become an assistant police chief in DC and then chief of police for the city of Richmond, VA); and John Thompson, who had played at Archbishop Carroll High School, Providence College, and with the NBA Boston Celtics.

The Kerlips had a group of run-and-shoot players who worked hard on defense to create turnovers, then run down the floor on the fast break for an easy lay-up or easy shot. These talents certainly aided us in our three consecutive DC Recreation Department City Championships. Gil Hoffman was a member of that team. He and Kermit Banks, the team player-coach, were teammates when they played basketball at Miner Teachers College. In addition to myself, other Kerlips players were Benjamin Metz, Frank Hart, James Cunningham, Fred "Rabbit" Gaskins, Harold Dean, Roosevelt James, Lynn Ring, Walt Kennedy, Jay Peterson, Donald Lipscomb, and my brother-in-law, Charles "Chuck" Baron.

Frank Hart was a starter on Armstrong High School's City and Conference Championship team in 1953. Rabbit Gaskins played with Frank Bolden at Cardozo High School and was a roving leader for the DC Recreation Department. Harold Dean was a former All-CIAA player for Virginia State College and coached Cardozo's 1966-67 Inter-High championship team. He would later return to his alma mater to coach and lead the Virginia State University Trojans basketball team to its 1988 CIAA Tournament Championship. Both Roosevelt James, who had played for me at Garnet Patterson, and Lynn Ring played for Harold when he was the basketball coach at Cardozo. Walt Kennedy played college ball at Florida A&M University in Tallahassee. He also played with the Harlem Globetrotters and coached locally at Coolidge and McKinley Tech high schools. Jay Peterson, who played high school basketball at Armstrong, and Donald Lipscomb were teammates of Sam Jones, the former Boston Celtics' star, when the three of them attended North Carolina College in the 1950s.

It was about this same period of time when I received an unexpected call from my friend Leo Miles, the head football and track coach at Bell Vocational High School. He called to tell me that Mr. Charles Baltimore, the principal at Bell who had also been a very successful basketball coach at Armstrong when I was playing for Dunbar, wanted to know the home basketball schedule for Garnet Patterson. I gave the information to Leo and was surprised to see Mr. Baltimore at our next home game. I knew him for many years but never called him anything other than Mr. Baltimore. We won the game, and Mr. Baltimore approached me at the end of the game to congratulate me. He asked me to give him a call soon. When I did call, he congratulated me again and told me he was interested in bringing me on board at Bell as a teacher and coach. He told me I would start out as an assistant coach in football, basketball, and track but would eventually, if all went well, become the head basketball coach. He asked if I would be interested. There was no doubt in my mind that this was something I was interested in, because one of my ambitions was to ultimately coach on the high-school level. My response to him was, "Definitely yes." He told me what I needed to do to make the transition, and I wasted no time at all.

In the meantime, Jimmy Coles, who was the basketball coach at Ballou, was asked by Mr. Carlo, the principal of Ballou, to give me a call. Jimmy told me he was leaving Ballou to go into administration and there would be a need to replace him as the basketball coach. He asked me to call Mr. Carlo. When I spoke with Mr. Carlo, he said he was interested in having me come to Ballou to teach and succeed Jimmy Coles as the head basketball coach there. I thanked him and asked if I could get back with him in a few days. I was thrilled to have been asked by both principals to join their staffs, but after considering both offers, I called Mr. Carlo to thank him and let him know that I had received a similar offer to coach at Bell and had decided to accept the offer from Mr. Baltimore.

Incidentally, Jimmy Coles had been a very good athlete in high school at Armstrong and later at Virginia State. Dr. James "Jimmy" Coles later became the first African-American principal at Wooten High School in Montgomery County, Maryland. The school's football stadium has been named in his honor.

After Leo was successful in coaching Bell to three straight Inter-High football championships, he coached football for one more year. After that he was promoted to assistant principal at Lincoln Junior High School, across the street from Bell. He had been very active as a football and basketball official for several years and became a head linesman in the NFL in 1969. He had the distinction of being the first African-American official to officiate a Super Bowl game. Leo officiated three Super Bowl games: Super Bowl VIII, X, and XIX.

In 1970 my wife, Tamara, who was working in the Student Personnel Division at Howard University, happened to be engaged in a conversation with Dr. Carl Anderson, the vice president for student activities. He knew I was involved with coaching and asked her if I might know someone who might be interested in becoming the athletic director at Howard. She shared that conversation with me at home that night, and I immediately thought of Leo. When I mentioned it to him he lit up with a smile and told me he was definitely interested in the job. This information was relayed to Dr. Anderson, who asked that Leo call to make an appointment for an interview. He did, and the rest is history. He became the athletic director at Howard in 1970 and remained in the position until 1986.

He continued to work as an NFL official during that time and beyond. When Jerry Seaman, the referee for the NFL officiating crew to which Leo was assigned, was promoted to become the director of the NFL officials in 1991, he asked Leo to join him as the supervisor of officials. Leo accepted the offer and moved to the NFL office in New York City. Leo held that position until his death in September 1995.

In the summer of 1966, I became the manager of Francis Swimming Pool, where I had worked as a lifeguard and water-safety instructor more than thirteen years before. One of my responsibilities as manager was to organize a rotation plan for the staff of lifeguards, who had to be visible and alert around the pools at all times. There were two pools – one small pool called the "baby pool" and a much larger pool 50 yards long and 20 yards wide with 4.5 feet depths at both ends and 11 feet deep in the middle. The three lifeguards scheduled to be on duty were assigned to man either one of the two lifeguard chairs or to patrol the deck around the two pools. They were required to be vigilant at all times and to be on the lookout for any possible dangers or potentially dangerous situations. If either lifeguard in one of the chairs had to leave his post (there were no female guards on staff) to make a swimming rescue, the lifeguard patrolling the deck was alerted to assume a position on the deck enabling him to see the smaller pool while also providing a backup for the larger pool until the swimmer was pulled to safety and determined not to be in need of further aid. These procedures were practiced routinely so that each lifeguard knew what his responsibility was if there were an emergency of this nature. Other supervisory responsibilities were to ensure the staff tested the pool water hourly to make certain the water met the Health Department regulations; to backwash or clean the filters helping to keep the water clear and clean; to make certain those using the pool followed the rules and regulations established for safety reasons; and to oversee locker room staff. During my time as a lifeguard, water-safety instructor, or manager there were some close calls, such as the incident with Petey Green back in the 1950s, and I did have to rescue several swimmers over the years. But I am proud to say that I never had a drowning or fatality on my watch.

That summer I was asked by Dr. Winston McAllister, Director of the Guyana Peace Corps Training Project which was being conducted on the campus of Howard University, to assist Coach Ted Chambers with the physical training activities for volunteers in the Project on a part-time basis. About that time, Vice President Hubert Humphrey had organized a program called Operation Champion which was involved in training inner-city youth to play and appreciate sports. He had invited a number of outstanding individuals from the field of sports to work with the youth in the inner city of Washington, DC. Among those individuals were Donna DeVarona and Wilma Rudolph. As the assistant physical education instructor in the Guyana Peace Corps Project, I was instrumental in bringing both Miss DeVarona and Miss Rudolph on campus to speak with the Peace Corps volunteers, with the assistance of Leo Miles, who was helping Vice President Humphrey with some aspect of the program.

Miss DeVarona visited the campus and spoke to the group about her background in swimming and her participation in the 1964 Olympics, where she won a gold medal in the 400-meter individual medley and 4x100-meter freestyle events. After answering a series of questions, she got into the swimming pool and gave a demonstration of the strokes and kicks she performed in the Olympics. In 1965 she became the first female sportscaster in television when she signed a contract with the American Broadcasting Company (ABC).

When Wilma Rudolph visited the Peace Corps volunteers, we met at the Banneker Stadium track across the street from the Howard University campus. Miss Rudolph, who had participated in the 1960 Olympics, told the volunteers she had suffered from polio, double pneumonia, and scarlet fever during her early childhood years. As a result of polio, she had to wear a steel brace on her right leg for a number of years. She was asked how she had overcome her disability, and she explained that she had received therapeutic massages at Meharry Medical College and from her family at home. As a result, she was able to discard the brace and ultimately began to walk normally. When she was in high school, she became an all-star performer in basketball. While attending Tennessee State University, she became a member of the track team and in 1960 won gold medals in the 100-meter dash, the 200-meter dash and the 4x100-meter relay as a member of the United States Olympic Track Team. In my view, she epitomized the determination, courage, perseverance, and attitude it took to overcome her own personal obstacles which may appear to have been almost insurmountable to many of us.

Miss Rudolph was a very attractive individual both physically and characteristically. She is a shining example of an individual who would not let what she could not do interfere with what she could do. This is advice that I have offered to my own children and grandchildren over the years. Wilma, like the mentally and physically challenged children with whom I worked as a lifeguard at Francis Swimming Pool years ago, like Gary Mays the one-armed baseball and basketball player from Armstrong High School and the individuals from so many foreign countries who participated in the International Deaf Olympics at the University of Maryland in College Park, saw a challenge and met it head on. Their achievements should send a message to those of us who are able bodied: In order to change the circumstances which may appear to be impediments in our lives, we need to stop complaining, stop looking for excuses, focus on our strengths rather than our weaknesses, and keep thinking positively.

The Operation Champion swimming competition was held at Banneker Swimming Pool, located at Georgia Avenue and College Street, Northwest. Several swimmers from the Francis Pool, including my three daughters, were entered in the events for their appropriate ages – 10 and under, 11 to 13, and 14 to 16. Terry, the oldest, was 12 and entered in the 50-yard backstroke, her specialty. Donna, who was 10 at the time, was entered in the 50-yard breaststroke. And Vicki, who was 8, entered the 50-yard freestyle. Terry won her event. Donna came in first in her event and won by such a wide margin that her closest competitor was at the midway point of the pool when she touched the finish line. Vicki came in first and all three, along with another swimmer from Francis, came in first in the medley relay. Vicki won a trophy for being the outstanding swimmer in her age group. This trophy sits in our recreation room among the many trophies members of our family have received over the years for their accomplishments in swimming, tennis, football, or basketball.

Around Washington during the spring and summer months, you could usually find loads of talented basketball players from this area engaged in games on the playground courts. One of the playgrounds frequented by youth of that era was Luzon, located at 13th and Van Buren streets, Northwest. On most Saturday and Sunday mornings and early afternoons, the two basketball courts were occupied with full-court, rise-and-fly, and first-team-to-score-30-points games. If you were playing 30 points and were the first team to reach that score, your team continued to play the next team waiting on the court. If your team lost, it might be four or five games before your team could rotate in to get another opportunity to play against a winning team. It would not be unusual to see high school or college coaches from the area watching the games in progress or even college coaches from out of town occasionally. They would sit on the hill overlooking the two basketball courts below and were in a position to see both games form their perches. The coaches were scouting, for the most part, hoping to find a basketball player or two whom they might be interested in recruiting for their school. They saw a lot of talented basketball players perform in those games. I recall seeing such coaches as Jim Lynam, from American University; Lefty Driesell from the University of Maryland; Herman Daves from Western High School; and Harold Dean from Cardozo, among others who attended on occasion.

On occasion while watching some of the weekend games, I invited several of the players who stood out to participate in a demonstration of their skills for the group of young people training for the Guyana Peace Corps Project on the campus of Howard University. Quite a few of them accepted my invitation, and I arranged to have the basketball court in Burr Gymnasium on Howard's campus reserved for this occasion. On the day of the demonstration, they were introduced to the trainees and then showed off their basketball skills in a scrimmage. Some of the players who participated were All-Metropolitan basketball players. They were Ed Epps, Cardozo; John Austin, DeMatha and Syracuse; Bernard Williams, DeMatha and LaSalle; Sid Catlett, DeMatha and Notre Dame; Bob Whitmore, DeMatha and Notre Dame; Collis Jones, St. John's College High School and Notre Dame; Austin Carr, Mackin and Notre Dame; Dave Bing, Spingarn and Syracuse; and John Thompson, Archbishop John Carroll High School and Providence College. The training process of the Guyana Peace Corps Project was rigorous because it was compacted into such a short period of time during that summer. But I would hope the activities provided through the physical education aspect of the project provided an opportunity for a change of venue and offered some degree of enjoyment and entertainment to the volunteers. The personal appearances of Donna DeVorona and Wilma Rudolph were well received and appreciated by the trainees. The same is true of the demonstrations provided by some of Washington's finest basketball players – they wowed all of us.

In the fall of that year, I assumed the position Mr. Baltimore had offered me at Bell Vocational High School. He assigned me to the positions of assistant football, assistant basketball, and assistant track coach. Leo Miles was the head football coach at the time, and two of his former teammates at Cardozo and Virginia State, Russell Williams and Ed Allen, both of whom I had played against in high school and college, were also his assistants, along with Julius Edmonson. Bell had already won the football Inter-High Championship the previous two years, 1964 and 1965. Some of the outstanding athletes of the day who played on those championship teams were Sam Singletary, tackle; Sylvester Gaines, end; Gilbert "Scrappy" Smith, halfback; Maurice Sutton, lineman; and Clark Douglas, end.

I was already familiar with many of the players, including Michael Jones, the quarterback in 1964, and Benjamin Wrenn, the quarterback during the 1965 and 1966 seasons, because I had taught them in junior high school at Garnet Patterson. Other former students of mine who were now student athletes at Bell were Larry Featherstone, John Bossard, Allen McDuffie, and Cole McIlwain.

After the 1966 championship football season at Bell, I began my assignment as an assistant to the head basketball coach, Richard "Moe" Janigan, and continued to work in this capacity through the 1968-69 basketball season. I was also the assistant track coach and had the privilege of working with Leo Miles, the head track coach. During the spring of 1969 I contacted Clarence "Bighouse" Gaines, the basketball coach and athletic director at Winston-Salem State College (now Winston-Salem State University), to talk with him about three very good athletes whom I thought he may be interested in. Each of these players, Franklin "Fat Cat" Jackson, Bobby Garner, and Carson Hankins, had played football at Bell. Jackson was a lineman, Garner was a 6'4" end, and Hankins at 6'4" was a quarterback. Garner and Hankins had also played basketball at Bell. All three received athletic scholarships to attend WSSC.

Other student athletes who had played at Bell during that time and received athletic scholarships to continue their education at postsecondary institutions were Robert Lee Stewart, Elizabeth City College; Sam Singletary and Gilbert Smith, North Carolina Central University; Clark Douglas, Colorado University; and Maurice Sutton, Norfolk State University.

Sutton was one of several young men from that era whose families included at least two generations of athletes. His wife, Gwendolyn, played basketball for North Carolina State University in Raleigh, NC. His daughter, Candice Sutton, played collegiately for the University of North Carolina at Chapel Hill. And his son, Maurice Sutton, Jr., played at Largo High School in Maryland and subsequently at Villanova University.

I had talked with Harold Hunter previously about the possibility of working with him as an assistant basketball coach at Tennessee State while taking a few graduate courses there toward a master's degree. I still had my GI Bill which I received when I was honorably discharged from the Army and could use to pay for my courses. Harold encouraged me to come to Tennessee to assist him and invited me to stay with him, if I chose to do so. I saw this as an opportunity to further my education while coaching on the college level and made preparations to enter Tennessee State as soon as Bell closed for the summer. It took me twelve hours, stopping only for gas and a snack, to drive from Washington, DC to Nashville. Once I had settled in on campus I began the registration process. Harold introduced me to a number of individuals on campus including Raymond Whitman, the athletic director; John Merritt, the head football coach; and Nolan "Super Nat" Smith, the former punt and kickoff return man for Tennessee State who was playing professionally for the Kansas City Chiefs at the time.

One day after class, I went by the Hunters and was surprised to see Wilma Rudolph who had stopped by to say hello to Harold and Jackie. She had just come in from Chicago, where she was living at the time, and was visiting Nashville for the day. I thanked her for visiting the Howard University Guyana Peace Corps Project a few years earlier to talk with the trainees in the project about her experiences. She was then, as she had been when I first met her, quite pleasant.

After classes I occasionally got a chance to workout and play basketball against Harold, Nolan, and some other athletes on the campus for the summer. After about five days, my mindset began to focus on my family back in Washington. I missed them more than I realized and began to be concerned about their welfare particularly without my being around. Nonetheless, I tried to continue to persevere in my classes, but after being on the campus for a little more than one full week – nine days to be exact – I had to admit to myself as well as to Harold how much I missed them and had become more and more concerned about their wellbeing. At that moment I had decided to return to Washington. I told him that I would be leaving the next day after I had dropped all of my classes. I thanked him for giving me the opportunity to work with him and for the chance to work on my graduate degree. The next day, as I was beginning my journey home, I stopped at a gasoline station near the campus to fill up my gas tank and check under the hood. As I was doing this, I saw John Merritt, the football coach. We spoke and I told him I was heading back to Washington because I missed my family and was concerned about them. He looked at me and said, "You big sissy." I smiled, shook his hand, and said goodbye. It took me eleven hours to get back home. It was such a relief to see my family again, even after such a short time of being away. It was unlike the separations we had experienced during the two years when I was in the Army, but perhaps it was in remembering those times that became the driving force to return home again.

After arriving home and seeing all was well and spending some quality time with my wife and children, I went to the Recreation Department to see if I could get my old job back as manager of the Francis Swimming Pool. I talked with Jim Tompkins, the aquatics director, and was told someone else had been assigned the task of managing the pool because I was not available when the pools opened for the summer. However, Jim told me that I could come onboard as a swimming pool supervisor if I were interested. In this position I would be one of three supervisors responsible for overseeing all of the public swimming pools operated by the Washington, DC Recreation Department. The other supervisors were James "Jim" Beiber and James "Jimmy" Dew.

There were twenty large swimming pools spread around the city in 1969 that we were assigned to supervise, plus fifteen walk-to pools being constructed that year. I was assigned the responsibility to check the progress of these walk-to pools as they were being completed and to make certain all of the equipment needed to operate the pools was in place prior to opening the pools to the public. Upon completion, one water-safety instructor and one lifeguard were assigned to each of the walk-to pools. The water-safety instructor was required to have a pool operator's permit certifying his qualification to operate the pool filtration system and oversee the welfare and safety of the swimmers. The walk-to pools were designed primarily for young children who had not learned to swim and also take some of the load off the larger pools. The walk-to pools were 40 feet long, 20 feet wide, and 4.5 feet deep. For security reasons, they were filled and emptied each day. The two individuals working at the pools worked an eight-hour day – two hours to fill the pool, an hour to teach swimming lessons, three hours for free swimming, and two hours to empty the pool. Some of the walk-to pools were Riggs-LaSalle, North Michigan Park, Deanwood, Barrie Farms, Benning Stoddert, J.O. Wilson, Watkins, Garrison, Lincoln Powell, Park View, Happy Hollow, Lincoln Capper, Kalarama, and Woodson. The twenty larger swimming pools were also located throughout the city. Located in the Northwest section of the city were Banneker, Cardozo, Dunbar, Francis, Georgetown, Takoma, and Upshur. In the Southwest section were East Potomac and Randall. In the Northeast section were Kelly Miller, Rosedale, H.D. Woodson, Langdon Park, and McKinley. And in the Southeast section were Anacostia, Barry Farms, Douglas, Fort Stanton, the Natatorium, and Oxon Run.

Several of the managers of the larger pools had made names for themselves in other sports as high school or college students. Stanley Gainor, the manager of the Cardozo pool, was an outstanding distance swimmer. He attended Tennessee State on a swimming scholarship and played tackle for Armstrong's football team in 1949 as a high school student. Bruce Bradford, the manager at H.D. Woodson and later at Rosedale, swam for Cardozo and Tennessee State. Kermit Banks, who managed Banneker, was a teammate of mine when we played on the 1948-49 basketball team at Dunbar. As mentioned earlier, Kermit also played on the basketball team at Miner Teachers College during the early 1950s and was the basketball coach for the Recreation Department's city championship teams in 1965, 1966, and 1967. Aaron Martin, the Barry Farms Swimming Pool manager, played football at my alma mater, North Carolina Central University, before playing professionally with the Philadelphia Eagles and the Washington Redskins. Ernest "Bull" Johnson, the manager of Kelly Miller, played football at North Carolina A&T University, coached football at Eastern High School, and became principal of Phelps Vocational High School. Edwin "Ed" Jones, the manager of Oxon Run, played football at North Carolina Central, coached football at Eastern High School, and became the principal of H.D. Woodson High School.

Incidentally, Loren Hill, the manager at Anacostia, is the brother of Darryl Hill, who was the first African-American to play football at the University of

Maryland. His mother, Mrs. Palestine Hill, and I taught at Garnet Patterson at the same time during the 1960s.

One of the highlights of the outdoor swimming pool season was the annual city-wide swimming meet. For this event, each of the twenty larger swimming pools in the city came under the supervision of the DC Recreation Department and entered teams to compete in the annual swimming meet. It was an opportunity for boys and girls all over the city to show off their swimming and diving skills and for managers of the pools to win bragging rights if their teams won. It attracted spectators from across the city – parents, siblings, aunts, uncles, and others who had an interest in the sport and who enjoyed good, healthy competition.

The swimming pool supervisors were responsible for the organization and the production of the swimming meet. The events were broken down by age-group categories, individual events, team relays, as well as stroke recognition such as breaststrokes, backstrokes, the American crawl or freestyle, and side stroke. Medals were awarded to the first-, second-, and third-place finishers. A trophy was awarded to the team that accumulated the highest total number of points.

After I was hired as a swimming pool supervisor, I told the aquatics director, Jim Tompkins, that I noticed the swimming pools did not have any visible signs on the deck or around the perimeter of the swimming pools to let the swimmers know what rules and regulations they were to abide by. He acknowledged that there were no written signs around the pools and agreed with me that it was very difficult to control the behavior of the swimmers if they were not aware of the rules and regulations established for their personal safety. I suggested that safety-awareness signs be posted at all of the pools to protect the safety of the swimmers and to protect those employees responsible for enforcing the rules. This, hopefully, would lessen the chance of injury and reduce the possibility of a fatality in the pool area. Jim acknowledged the immediate necessity for these signs and authorized a work order requesting the rules and regulations governing the behavior of all swimmers be placed in all of the pools throughout the city.

Some time later Jim asked me to become the troubleshooter among the swimming pool supervisors. He had received several calls from some of the personnel working at the new Oxon Run Swimming Pool; the employees were complaining about their manager, Ed Jones. Jim asked me to go to the Oxon Run Swimming Pool, located in the far southeastern section of the District of Columbia, to see what was going on. I arrived there around 11:30 in the morning, just as they were closing down for the morning swim session and prior to the time when pool personnel would normally break for lunch. Ed Jones acknowledged my presence and asked all of the pool personnel to take chairs out to the pool deck and be seated. He sat down behind them, and I walked to the front of the group. I introduced myself and told them I was one of the swimming pool supervisors for the Recreation Department. I said I was there because the director of aquatics had received several calls from one or more individuals employed at Oxon Run complaining about the management of the pool under the direction of Mr. Jones. I listened to several individuals express their concerns and complaints about the manner in which they were being supervised. It seemed Mr. Jones required all of the employees to assume the responsibility to keep the pool area clean and free from any safety hazards inside and out. They complained that he was constantly finding things for them to do. And as a result, they had built up a hostile and negative attitude toward him. After listening to them vent their frustrations and anger, I asked, "Who has the best swimming pool in the city?" All of them responded in unison, "We do." I asked, "Who has the cleanest swimming pool in the city?" And again they responded, "We do." Then I said that they could not have the best swimming pool or the cleanest if Ed did not do his job in getting all of them to do the various things needed to make Oxon Run the best pool in the city. I further pointed out to them that whether they realized it or not, they had complimented Ed. "It's good to know," I said, "that he is doing the job he was hired to do – managing and operating a clean and safe pool for the swimmers and getting all of the employees, who are paid for every minute while here, to do the work required." The staff is a team, I told them, and Ed is the coach of this team. I emphasized again that they were getting paid for every minute they were there and if they were not happy working there, they had the right to seek employment elsewhere. I reported back to Jim Tompkins after the meeting at Oxon Run and told him the employees were actually complimenting Ed Jones by letting me know he was doing the job he was sent there to do by insisting that they do theirs.

It was the first week in September, and the swimming pools traditionally closed the first Monday in September. The summer help was comprised mostly of individuals who were still in school, and schools would be opening soon for the fall. Those who staffed the locker rooms were high school students, and the lifeguards and water-safety instructors were in college or employed in the school system, for the most part. I reported back to work at Bell Vocational High School as a teacher and coach. When I went to the principal's outer office to sign the teachers' attendance sheet, I was told by Mr. Baltimore's secretary that he wanted to see me after I signed in. I did so and went in to see him. He greeted me and asked how my summer had been. I told him about my trip to Tennessee and my objective for going there but that I had changed my mind and returned home. He said he was glad to know everything had gone well and that he had some good news for me. "I'm appointing you to be the head basketball and head track coach," he said. I lit up with a big smile and thanked him. Not only was I happy about becoming the head coach of the basketball and track teams, but I would actually be paid for coaching –something I had wanted for years.

Mr. Baltimore had served on a long-standing committee with the task to consider a plan for paying high school coaches in the city schools. When their task was completed, their recommendation to the school board was that high school coaches be paid for their efforts. Mr. Baltimore had been a very successful high school coach at Armstrong Technical High School, and coaches weren't being paid during his tenure of coaching.

I was really excited about becoming the head basketball coach at Bell because I viewed it as a challenge. First, Bell had the second smallest enrollment among the public high schools in Washington – only Chamberlain, another vocational high school, had a smaller enrollment. This meant I would not have as many students to come out for the team as other schools with larger enrollments and the competition to make the team would not be as great. Secondly, Bell's gym was smaller than a regulation junior high school basketball court. This meant we would have to improvise during practice if our players were to be able to make adjustments when we played on a regulation high school court. On a regulation court, the court is longer and wider than the court at Bell where we practiced.

The year prior to my becoming the head basketball coach, Mr. Baltimore, having been a very successful high school basketball coach himself, realized the disadvantage of not having a regulation basketball court. In an attempt to resolve the problem, he initiated a conversation with Mr. Fields, the principal of Lincoln Junior High School at the time, about the possibility of having the gym floor at Lincoln lengthened to the standards for a regulation high school court. Then Bell would have access to a nearby regulation court when the gym was not being used by faculty and students at Lincoln. Lincoln was directly across the street from Bell on Hiatt Place. Mr. Baltimore assured Mr. Fields that if he were willing to alter the court, he would raise the money to have the work done. Lines would have to be redrawn on the floor, the basketball goals would have to be moved back, and a scoreboard would have to be installed. After further discussions about this and other options, the two of them checked with administrators in the DC Public Schools front office to see if there were any reasons to prevent them from moving forward with their plan. There were none. They were given permission to move forward with their plans, and the changes were made.

On the first day of school for teachers and administrators in the fall of 1968, we received organizational tasks assigned by the principal. Students began coming to school the next day. School had been in session for about a week when I made an announcement for students who were interested in playing on the basketball team to meet with me in the school gym. Richard Mosby, one of the physical education teachers, agreed to work with me as the assistant basketball coach. About twenty students attended the meeting. I told them we would hold tryouts for two days and have five-on-five scrimmages, with the two winning teams playing each other. The first team to reach 20 points would be the winner.

I conveyed to them that Coach Mosby and I were looking for individuals who could demonstrate not only offensive skills such as ball handling, dribbling, the ability to make lay-ups and foul shots, outside shooting, and passing ability, but good defensive skills as well, such as aggressiveness, the ability to intercept passes, guard players on the other team, steal balls, block shots, get rebounds, and so on.

At the conclusion of the second day of scrimmage, I put up a list of the individuals who would be invited out for the school team. The next day I met with all of the fellows who had been chosen for the team. There were only three players from the previous Bell basketball team returning. One of those three had been voted by the 1968-69 team to be captain during the 1969-70 basketball season. I explained to them I was changing the philosophy to a defensive run-and-shoot style of play and we would put a lot of emphasis on the defensive aspect of the game by playing aggressively – causing turnovers, making steals, interceptions, running, and passing the ball down the floor before the opposition has a chance to set up defensively on the opposite end of the court. This would enable us to make easy lay-up shots. I assured them that no team would be in better physical condition than we would be because I was putting a lot of emphasis on physical conditioning, and I wanted all of them to be on the cross country team to help get them in good condition before we started basketball practice. My promise to them was: If they worked hard, became assertive, mastered the fundamentals that we would be working on in daily practice, got good grades, and stayed out of trouble, I would get them into college. The caveat was that the college, whether it was a junior college or four-year college, would depend on their academic standing in high school as well as their standardized test scores.

When the meeting ended, the young man who had been voted captain of the team came up to me and said, "I'm not going to run cross country." I was somewhat taken aback but regained my composure and told him he was expected to show leadership by example as captain of the team, to set a positive image for the rest of the team. He rolled his eyes and again said he was not going to run cross country. I looked at him and said, "Then that means that you will not be on the team." He rolled his eyes once more and walked away. At that moment I felt the need to make a point to the rest of the team that not following the directives from the coaches and displaying a negative attitude would not be tolerated, even if the individual happened to be the captain of the team. Suffice it to say, that individual did not remain on the Bell Vocats basketball team.

When we began basketball practice, it was usually after school. Classes ended at 3:00 P.M., and members of the basketball team were expected to be in the Bell gym by 3:15 P.M. Practice was usually held in the Bell gym unless the gym at Lincoln was not being utilized. For fifteen minutes, they were to work out individually at three stations with the Exer-Genies, climb ropes to the top of the gym, and then shoot around until 3:30 P.M., when all of the players were expected to be present. At that point, we collectively began our exercise regimen. Because the Bell gym was so small, we had to improvise to help the players get in condition. We had the players run in place for five minutes and sprint at an accelerated pace for the last minute, followed by shooting foul shots while they were still winded. That was followed by another five-minute period of running in place with their hands on the wall, then stopping to shoot foul shots while still winded. This was followed by a series of exercises such as:

A. The side straddle hop (30 four-count repetitions)
B. High jumper (30 four-count repetitions)
C. Squat thrust (30 four-count repetitions)
D. Arm circles (30 four-count repetitions)
E. Leg lifts
F. Pushups

G. Running in place (30 four-count repetitions with a speed-up count at 20)
H. Stagger step-wide base, low center (running in place, front, right, back, left, etc.)
I. Quick step (running, twisting legs right and left, head straight) backward
J. Bench jumping
K. Altman jumps – touch basket, backboard, and strings

All of the exercises were done to stress the development of posture and muscles needed to execute the various positions and situations they would find themselves in during an actual basketball game. The following fundamentals of basketball were practiced regularly except on game days:

A. Boxers shuffle (around the perimeter of the court with a wide stance, low center)
B. Pivoting drill (team up, one player attempts to take the ball)
C. Dribbling drill
D. Tapping drill (off the backboard)
E. Rebounding drill
F. Box-out drill
G. Passing drill (chest pass, softball pass, baseball pass, two-hand overhead pass, and hook pass)
H. Weave (five minutes)
I. Figure Eight down and back
J. Fast break defense (3 on 2)
K. Little man-big man guards – forward, center, outlet drill
L. Rebound outlet pass drill (half-court pass)
M. Shooting drill (done while dribbling)

1. Lay-up, right hand
2. Crossover under basket, left hand
3. Crossover jumper from corner
4. Crossover jumper from outlet area
5. Double crossover jumper at foul line
6. Straight down jumper at foul line
7. Straight in lay-up
8. Repeat all of the above on left side, using left hand

The length of time spent on the execution of fundamentals was reduced as the players began to master them. Some of the principles I stressed in playing individual defense were:

1. Never turn your back on the basketball
2. Find out if the person you are guarding is right-handed or left-handed
3. Don't let the person you are guarding have the position he wants
4. Sag toward the middle and the basket when the ball is away from you and the person you are guarding
5. Never let your man get between you and the basket
6. Make the person dribbling the ball go where you want him to go
7. When the person away from you dribbles the ball with his back toward you, double-team or trap him
8. The baselines, sidelines, and half-court lines are trapping areas
9. If the person you are guarding beats you off the dribble, try to reach around him and deflect the ball
10. Go over the top with the ball when the person you are guarding tries to run you into a screen
11. If you know you are beaten on a screen, holler "switch" to your teammate, assist him in making the switch by placing your hand on his hip and pushing him toward the person you are guarding
12. Always protect the basket
13. Never cross your legs when playing defense
14. Keep your arms up and hands moving

Bell's starting lineup consisted of two sophomores, two juniors, and one senior. Jesse Smith, a 6' guard, and Gregory "Greg" Carrington, a 6'3" center, were the two sophomores. Kenneth "Kenny" Barnes, a 6' guard, and Thomas "Tom" Tobias, a 6'3" forward, were the two juniors, and Larry Holloway, a 5'6" guard, was the one senior in the starting lineup.

Before the season began, I emphasized to the team that we would be awarding individual trophies at the end of the season in three areas. One would be to the most valuable player based on several characteristics: Demonstrated leadership qualities, a positive attitude on and off the court, determination and perseverance throughout the game, and a combination of offensive and defensive statistics compiled after each game. The second trophy would be awarded to the outstanding offensive player on the team based on statistics kept by the team manager during each game, including assists (passing from a teammate leading to a basket), offensive rebounds, lay-ups made or missed, outside shooting made or missed, and foul shots made or missed. The third trophy would be awarded to the outstanding defensive player based on the individual's ability to block shots, get defensive rebounds, double-team, intercept passes, offensive charges, stolen balls, and jump balls. To put more emphasis on the defensive aspect of basketball, I made a large chart with the above categories printed in bold lettering and even larger bold lettering on the top of the charts naming the defensive player of the week. I put a large 8x10 picture on the chart of the player who earned the title along with his name under the picture and put the chart in a showcase near the main office so that the faculty and student body would recognize the player and congratulate him. This gesture seemed to further motivate the players who received this recognition because they became better known and popular with the students as well as the faculty and staff. My intent was to motivate the entire basketball team to strive for more defensive plays during each game. With our defensive scheme, I implemented a man-to-man full-court and a half-court press. I also put in various zone defenses, such as a 2-1-2 half-court and full-court, and 3-2 half-court and full-court. From these formations we could put pressure on the ball handler by trapping or double-teaming him, frequently causing the ball handler to turn the ball over to the defense and leading to quick or easy baskets for the Bell Vocats.

I assigned numbers to our defensive sets. Any set of numbers ending in zero meant we were employing a full-court defense. Any set of numbers ending in five meant we were employing a half-court defense. Any set of numbers where the first two digits are alike meant we would employ a man-to-man defense. For instance, if I called out any of the following numbers 110, 220, 330, 440, or 550, each of them would mean the same thing – man-to-man full-court defense. If I called out 115, 225, 335, 445, or 555, each meant the team would go into a man-to-man half-court defense. When I called for a zone defense, I simply doubled the numbers. For instance, when I wanted the team to set up in a full-court zone press, I called out 640, which would actually be a 3-2 full-court zone press. I doubled the first two numbers, double three is six and double two is four and the last digit zero meant full-court. Therefore, the number 640 would be a 3-2 full-court press. I used the number system in practice, and when I saw any of the players in the halls at school, between classes, or during recess and called out "645," for example, I expected a quick response of "3-2 half-court." I reminded the team frequently that not only did they represent Bell, the school, themselves, and their families, but just as importantly, they represented me, and I expected them to always conduct themselves like gentlemen: no rowdiness on or off the basketball court in school or away from school. If they were caught in a negative situation, they could very well be removed from the team. I emphasized that I did not want to hear any member of the team using profanity at any time. I pointed out to them that they had never heard me use profanity. It was not necessary because it was not what you say that is significant but how you say it. The penalty for using profanity was to chew a piece of soap to serve as a deterrent and a reminder for future behavior, hopefully. I recognize this was a different time and age in our society and what could be and was done then, in our attempt as teachers and coaches to mold the character of our youth, could not be considered in today's society.

The Inter-High league was divided into two divisions – the East Division and the West Division, with seven teams making up each division. The East Division included Anacostia, Ballou, Chamberlain, McKinley, Phelps, Spingarn, and Woodson. In the West Division were Bell, Cardozo, Coolidge, Dunbar, Roosevelt, Western, and Wilson.

Bell's basketball schedule for the 1969-70 school year began in December. Games scheduled during the month of December were usually against teams from the District of Columbia Inter-High East Division teams or against high schools located outside the city. At the end of December, Bell had played five basketball games – four of the games were against teams from the Inter-High East Division. We split with those teams, winning 2 and losing 2. The fifth game was played against the Bell alumni, and we won that game. In the first four games, we averaged 90.2 points per game.

Bell's roster for that year included the following players:

Name	Position	Height	Weight	Classification
Barnes, Kenneth	Guard	6'0"	158	Junior
Carrington, Gregory	Center	6'3"	175	Sophomore
Carter, Calvin	Guard	5'10"	153	Senior
Davis, Cornell	Guard	5'9"	165	Senior
Davis, Robert	Forward	6'1"	175	Junior
Holloway, Larry	Guard	5'6"	145	Senior
Paul, Arthur	Guard	5'7"	145	Junior
Smith, Jesse	Guard	6'0"	155	Junior

Tobias, Thomas	Forward	6'3"	205	Junior
Williams, Billy	Forward	5'11"	180	Junior

My assistant coach was Richard E. Mosby, and the managers of the team were Robert Hunter and Ronald Dinkins.

Chapter 8

THE BELL VOCATS in the Western Division of the District of Columbia Inter-High Athletic Association (DCIAA) were scheduled to play each of the schools in their division twice; normally, on a home-and-home basis unless one or both teams did not have a home court. In a situation where a team did not have a home court, the games were scheduled to be played on a neutral court.

Our first game in our division was scheduled against the Coolidge Colts – a team with a definite height advantage over us, but I did not think they were as quick or as fast as we were. Their center was Glenn Price, a 6'9" All-Metropolitan player. Rodney Carr, the younger brother of Alston Carr, was 6'4". And Bradford Tatum at 6'2" was the son of the former DC Recreation Department official by the same name and the nephew of John Tatum. Senior Bradford Tatum and John Tatum were both widely acclaimed swimmers, having won countless medals in the National Senior Olympics in swimming, an event held annually. John Tatum's son, Kevin, played point guard for McKinley Tech and was a sportswriter for *The Philadelphia Inquirer*.

Our tallest players were Gregory Carrington and Thomas Tobias, both 6'3". We were not successful in stopping Glenn Price in the game because he scored 42 points against us. However, we were able to get our fast break going. Greg and Tom Tobias were doing a very good job of rebounding, boxing out, and getting the basketball out to the outlet area to start our fast break. Larry Holloway, who was only 5'6" tall but very quick, scored 32 points following Carrington's 25 points to help lead Bell over Coolidge. The final score was Bell 95, Coolidge 80.

Our second division game that year was against Western High School. Robert "Bob" Piper was also in his first year as Western's basketball coach, as I was at Bell. Piper was an All-South Western Athletic Conference (SWAC) basketball player when he played for his alma mater, Grambling University. He attended Grambling when Eddie Robinson, the outstanding football coach and athletic director, was there. He also played professionally in the American Basketball Association (ABA).

Western started the game by leading Bell 16-0 before the Vocats scored. At halftime, Western was leading by 10 points, 36-26. In our desire and determination to turn things around, the Vocats turned up the defensive pressure to man-to-man full-court, causing Western to make many mistakes. The man-to-man full-court pressure caused Western's players to make back-court violations, traveling violations, and throw intercepted passes. Bell's trapping, double-teaming press caused a number of turnovers, allowing Bell to make a number of easy lay-ups off fast-break situations. Because of the full-court pressure applied on defense, Bell lost five players as they fouled out of the game. Western led for the first 30.5 minutes, but Bell came out victorious in the end by the score of 84-80.

When the game was over and it dawned on me that we had won after coming back from a 16-0 start and a 10-point deficit at halftime, I became quite emotional and broke out in tears of sheer joy. When the team returned to the locker room, I praised them for their efforts, strong will, determination, and perseverance. I said, "I hope you will be able to carry this will-to-win with you throughout the rest of our games and later on in life, because life will present you with many challenges and obstacles. During those times, you will need the same kind of effort, will, and determination to overcome those obstacles. Remember, a winner never quits and a quitter never wins. Hopefully the effort you demonstrated in this game will be carried over into other real-life situations."

Later on during the same basketball season, we played Western again. Western was leading at halftime 38-30. In the fourth quarter (high school basketball games are played for a total of 32 minutes in 8-minute quarters), we again applied our full-court man-to-man press and once again came out winners with a score of 74-65. With this, I repeated one of my favorite quotes: "A winner never quits and a quitter never wins."

We went on to complete our basketball schedule and finished the season with a record of 11 wins and 9 losses. With this accomplishment, I felt the seeds had been planted for the type of basketball philosophy I was trying to implement. I realized that in implementing an up-tempo or fast-break method with a young ball club, the likelihood that the ball would be turned over frequently during the course of a game would certainly increase. However, I expected to see a much improved team during the 1970-71 basketball season with continued intense practice.

After the completion of the regular season and the Inter-High championship game, I was asked to coach a group of senior all-stars from the Inter-High West Division in a game against a group of senior all-stars from the Inter-High East Division. The game, played at McKinley Tech, was a benefit for the Boys Club of Greater Washington (BCGW). Some of the players who performed for the West Division team were Glenn Price and Rodney Carr of Coolidge; David Lewis and Milton Lundy of Roosevelt; and Cornell Davis, Larry Holloway, and Joe Cunningham of Bell. To our delight, the game was won by the West Division All-Stars.

In April of that year, McKinley Armstrong, the basketball coach at McKinley Tech, and I took an All-Metropolitan basketball team from the Washington Metro area to the 1970 Philadelphia Youth Athletic Association (PYAA) Four Cities Basketball Tournament. The tournament was held at the Spectrum arena. Other teams participating in that tournament were South Jersey, New York City, and, of course, the hometown team, Philadelphia.

Two of the players on New York's team were Len Elmore and "Jap" Trimble. These two individuals eventually ended up playing basketball for Charles "Lefty" Drisell at the University of Maryland in College Park. After graduation, Len Elmore played basketball in the NBA for a number of years. After his basketball playing days were over, he attended Harvard Law School and obtained his law degree. He more recently can be seen and heard as a sports analyst on ESPN and CBS television.

Howie Evans, the coach of the Metro Team from New York, was a sportswriter for the New York-based *New Amsterdam News*. Howie later took a leave of absence and returned to his alma mater, the University of Maryland Eastern Shore in Princess Anne, to coach the men's basketball team there.

Representing the Washington Metro All-Stars were Glenn Price of Coolidge; Stanley Washington of Spingarn; Embee Shaw and Willie Daniels of Eastern; David Lewis, Milton Lundy and Billy Lee of Roosevelt; Eugene Oliver and Kermit Ellis of Fairmont Heights; Johnny Lloyd of Anacostia; James Buckmon and Haywood Corley of McKinley; and Cornell Davis of Bell. In our first match-up, we played the home team, Philadelphia, and won. The score was Washington 89, Philadelphia 82. The leading scorers for our team were Eugene Oliver with 28 points and Stanley Washington with 18 points.

South Jersey defeated New York in the other game that night, so we played South Jersey in the final. We defeated South Jersey in the championship game 73-71. Eugene Oliver was our leading scorer with 17 points, and he was also selected as the tournament's most valuable player. This concluded the 1969-70 basketball season for us.

Stanley Washington went on to play for Coach Bernie Bickerstaff on the college level at San Diego State. Both of them ultimately joined forces with the Washington Bullets – Stanley as a player and Bernie as an assistant coach. Bernie later became assistant coach and head coach with several NBA teams.

As we approached the 1970-71 basketball season, I had high hopes the Bell Vocats would return with a new and positive sense of accomplishment. Having gone through the 1969-70 basketball season as an inexperienced team adjusting to a new system and philosophy, I hoped that another year would be meaningful in bringing more wins to the team. Richard Mosby continued to work with me as my assistant, and our managers that year included Robert Hunter, Ronald Dinkins, Ernest Crawford, and Charles Walker.

Four of our starting lineup players from the previous year returned. They were seniors Kenny Barnes and Tom Tobias; juniors Jesse Smith and Greg Carrington; and an incoming sophomore Webster Jordan. Jordan was a very quick 6'1" point guard. The following is a list of Bell's roster for 1970-71:

Name	Position	Height	Weight	Classification
Barnes, Kenneth	Guard	6'0"	158	Senior
Blake, Larry	Guard	5'10"	147	Junior
Carr, Carlton	Guard	5'9"	155	Sophomore
Carrington, Gregory	Center	6'4"	180	Junior
Cloyd, James	Guard	5'9"	155	Sophomore
Davis, Robert	Forward	6'2"	180	Senior
Donaldson, Tyrone	Forward	6'3"	185	Sophomore
Harrison, Howard	Guard	5'10"	147	Sophomore
Jordan, Webster	Guard	6'1"	175	Sophomore
Long, Gerald	Center	6'7"	185	Senior
Smith, Jesse	Guard	6'0"	155	Junior
Tobias, Thomas	Forward	6'4"	210	Senior
Williams, Billy	Forward	6'0"	185	Senior
Wright, Cleo	Forward	6'2"	155	Sophomore

We were victorious in our first five scheduled basketball games against inter-city foes, Chamberlain, Phelps, and Spingarn, and in two away games against Atlantic City High and Addison High in Roanoke, Virginia. The Vocats next scheduled game was against Coach Herman Daves and his team, the Ballou Knights. This was our home game played at Lincoln Junior High School. Ballou led at halftime 39-30 behind the scoring of the Campbell brothers, Charles and Randolph. With time running out, less than a minute to play in the game, and Bell leading by one point, 76-75, I called timeout. It was customary for Bell players on the bench when timeout was called to relinquish their seats to those players coming off the court to allow them a brief moment to get off their feet. With all of the players huddled around, I gave the team the game situation at hand: "We have less than a minute to play, and we have a one point lead. Let's go into a four-corners semi-stall, and the only kind of shot we want is a lay-up." I repeated myself, "The only kind of shot we want is a lay-up." Then I asked the team to repeat what I had said. The response was given in unison, "A lay-up." Then I said, "Don't turn the ball over!"

We had possession of the ball as the game continued. After the ball was thrown inbounds, we immediately went into a four-corners formation. The ball was passed into the left corner near the baseline and caught by our player positioned there. Instead of trying for a lay-up, he immediately shot a jumper and missed. I am certain that my expression at that moment said it all; there was no need to verbalize what I was thinking. A Ballou player rebounded the ball and quickly passed the ball down court to one of his teammates, who shot the ball and made the basket. Shortly after that, on another play, a Ballou player was fouled. He made the two free-throws, and the game was over. Ballou had won with a final score of 79-76. We lost that game because one individual failed to follow instructions. We played Ballou again in the Inter-High Christmas Tournament and Ballou won again, 86-68.

As the season progressed, I realized how much work we had to do. Oftentimes, some of our players found themselves jumping in the air but unsure whether to pass the ball or shoot it. In situations such as this, we frequently turned the ball over. To minimize the frequency of these kinds of situations, they were told to either throw or shoot the ball at the basket because there is a fifty-fifty chance of the ball going into the basket and no chance if the ball were intercepted. This advice would pay off later in the season. They were also told that as hard as they practiced and worked at running our offense, they would one day put on a clinic on how to break another team's full-court pressure defense and change it into fast-break situations leading to easy baskets. With lots of practice, that did happen in a future game.

My job required that I not only work with the players on honing basketball skills but also on changing attitudes that often got in the way of our ability to move forward. After much discussion among the coaching staff, it was decided that a series of consequences for players who displayed negative attitudes and behavior would be implemented. I had placed a lot of emphasis on the need to follow instructions, and there were times when the inability of a single individual to follow instructions impacted on the entire team, unfortunately. The rationale followed what we had seen in the game against Ballou: When one individual failed to follow the game plan, the whole team suffered the consequence. Having the entire team involved in running laps because of noncompliance on the part of a fellow player usually led to a reprimand on the offending player by the rest of the team. Hopefully, this would lessen the probability of the same thing happening again.

I also placed an emphasis on conditioning. The importance of being able to change one's mindset when fatigue set in required a great deal of conditioning of both the mind and the body. To prove my point, I told the team if they had to play ten consecutive basketball games, run around the block fifteen times, and then play two more games, they would probably say, "Coach, I can't move any more. I'm too tired." But if, at that moment, a big lion appeared and was coming straight toward them, I assured them they would find enough energy to get up and run. So, one could say tiredness is a state of mind. Hopefully, this lesson would have some carryover value later on in their lives. For I am quite certain that for each of them, there would be situations arising in their lives when they may feel they cannot put one foot in front of the other – it may be job or family related – but if they are compelled to get it done, they would find a way.

The Vocats went on to have a successful regular season against the Inter-High Western Division teams that year. We won both of our scheduled games against Coolidge, Western, and Wilson and split the games with Cardozo, Dunbar, and Roosevelt. Going into the Inter-High playoff, Bell defeated Cardozo for the right to face Ballou in the Inter-High championship playoffs. Ballou was rated number one in the metropolitan area for much of the 1970-71 season. They were known for their full-court 3-2 zone press, and they had the Campbell brothers, Charles and Randolph, who were both All-Metropolitan basketball players.

The game was played at McKinley Tech. Just before the game began, Tom Young, the head basketball coach at American University, and his assistant coach, Dr. Tom Davis, took seats just behind our bench where they could see and hear everything said and done by me and my assistant coach. At the beginning of the game, we jumped to an early lead with a score of 14-2. Ballou began using their full-court 3-2 zone press after they made a basket, and we made shambles of their press. Quickly taking the ball out of bounds and making quick short passes, we broke the press and scored 2 points at the other end of the court without the basketball touching the floor. Bell held a 62-43 halftime lead.

During the second half, Ballou attempted to pressure us all over the court. This tactic resulted in Ballou fouling a lot and sending us to the free-throw line, where we converted most of our shots. At one point in the second half, Billy Williams, one of our players who was near the outlet area and right-side lane, was about to make a pass to a teammate and committed himself by jumping into the air to make the pass. Immediately, he realized that his teammate was covered and if he made the pass, it would have led to a turnover and Ballou would gain possession of the basketball. Billy elected to throw the ball at the basket while he was still in the air and off balance, and the ball went in. At that point, I thought there was no way we could lose that game. Fortunately, Bell won the game 112-91.

By winning the playoff game against Ballou, Bell's next opponent was McKinley Tech. This game was played for the Inter-High Championship in Burr Gymnasium on the campus of Howard University on a sunny afternoon. There was a capacity crowd in attendance. Bell was leading at halftime 32-29. When we returned to the court after halftime, the sun was shining brightly on the basket at the south end of the court, where Bell was shooting during the second half. The sun was not a factor during the first half of the game when McKinley was shooting at the basket. However, it did present a problem for our players, because there was a consistent glare on the glass backboard. Late in the ball game, one of our players missed two lay-ups he probably would have made had there not been a glare on the basket. McKinley rebounded the missed shots, took possession of the ball, and made two quick and easy shots and won the game. The two shots we missed and the two baskets they made were the game changers – the final score was 71-66. Although both teams played well, McKinley came out on top.

Greg Carrington was selected as the Most Valuable Player in the Inter-High playoff tournament. Bell played well enough to have had a season record of 17 wins and 6 losses. We went over the century mark five times that season against Inter-High opposition with the following scores:

Bell 107Chamberlain 75
Bell 104Coolidge 85
Bell 104Wilson 65
Bell 102Coolidge 73
Bell 112Ballou 91

Several weeks later, I received a letter from Dr. Tom Davis dated April 5, 1971, congratulating me for an outstanding season (see exhibit). Tom left American University to become the head basketball coach at Lafayette College in Easton, Pennsylvania. He later coached at Boston College, Stanford University, and Iowa University.

Jesse Smith and Greg Carrington were Bell's co-captains for the 1970-71 season. Both of them exhibited leadership through example and were selected to the Inter-High West First Team. Carrington was also selected to the All-Metropolitan First Team. Some of the other talented basketball players in the Inter-High league who Bell played against or whom I had the privilege to see play were Alonzo Patterson and Wilbur Thomas of Roosevelt; Michael Riley and DeCarlo Wiley of Cardozo; Keith Byrd of Dunbar; Cornell Robinson of Western; Charles and Randolph Campbell and William Parker of Ballou; James Monroe, Jeffrey Harrison and Lonnie Perrin of McKinley; Walter Chesley of Eastern; William Lynn of Spingarn; Kenneth Kee of Phelps; and Glenn Price of Coolidge.

Lonnie Perrin was also an outstanding football player; he received a football scholarship to play at the University of Illinois. After college, he played in the NFL for several years with the Denver Broncos.

In the spring of 1971 after the regular season had ended, I received a telephone call from Sam Jones, the basketball coach at Federal City College. Sam told me that Kenny Hudson, an NBA official, and Tom "Satch" Sanders, his former teammate with the Boston Celtics, were interested in bringing an All-Metropolitan basketball team from Boston down to Washington to play an All-Metropolitan team from Washington. They were wondering if Sam knew someone who could arrange to make this happen. I agreed to see what I could do. I began calling a few coaches to see if they would let their players represent Washington and their teams in playing against the team from Boston. I got a lot of cooperation from each of the coaches I contacted. McKinley

Armstrong agreed to work with me as the assistant coach of the Washington team and arranged to have us practice at McKinley Tech. I had difficulty finding a site for the game and finally contacted my brother, Leon, the principal at Roper Junior High at the time. He was willing to accommodate us, but because the District of Columbia Recreation Department was scheduled to use the Roper gymnasium at the time and date we needed the gym for the game, he needed to get a clearance from them. After some negotiating, I received permission to use the facilities with the stipulation that I could not charge admission to the game.

The game was scheduled and received favorable publicity form the local newspapers. Representing the DC team were Lonnie Perrin, Jeffrey Harrison, and James Monroe of McKinley Tech; Charles and Randolph Campbell of Ballou; Adrian Dantley of DeMatha; Greg Carrington, Jesse Smith, and Webster Jordan of Bell; Kenneth Kee of Phelps; and Wilbur Thomas of Roosevelt. When the team from Boston arrived, they were accompanied by another former Boston teammate of Sam's, K.C. Jones. The capacity crowd was treated to some phenomenal basketball. Charles Campbell was high-point man with 31 points. Adrian Dantley almost single-handedly took over the game in the last few minutes, giving the Washington team the winning score of 100 to Boston's 93.

After such a successful and eventful basketball season, it was disappointing to begin our track season with what appeared to be little interest on the part of the student body. There was such limited interest and participation that I encouraged members of the football and basketball teams to take part by emphasizing how beneficial it would be to them in their respective sports – throwing the shot-put would enhance an individual's strength and running would help improve and increase their speed and quickness. We did compete in dual meets against other high schools such as Chamberlain, Dunbar, and Cardozo, but did not have enough participants who could compete successfully with the top trackmen in the Inter-High at that point.

We entered the 1971-72 basketball season with great expectations. We had played McKinley for the Inter-High Championship the previous season in a very competitive game and were expecting a number of our players from that game to return to Bell the next year. Given this, we were enthusiastic about our chances for another successful season, and this enthusiasm was shared by the players themselves. The Bell Vocats team roster for that year was as follows:

Name	Position	Height	Weight	Classification
Anderson, Leslie	Forward	6'3"	182	Sophomore
Battles, Donald	Guard	5'11"	160	Junior
Carrington, Gregory	Center	6'4"	185	Senior
Combs, Charles	Forward	6'1"	162	Sophomore
Dennis, Desmond	Forward	6'5"	206	Sophomore
Harrison, Howard	Guard	6'0"	148	Sophomore
Jordan, Webster	Guard	6'1"	182	Junior
Smith, Jesse	Guard	6'0"	158	Senior
Tate, John	Guard	6'0"	147	Sophomore
Tharpe, Larry	Center	6'5"	190	Sophomore
Tibbs, Ronald	Guard	5'9"	140	Sophomore
Washington, Gary	Guard	5'11"	170	Sophomore
Whitmyer, Barry	Guard	5'11"	190	Sophomore
Wright, Cleo	Forward	6'3"	167	Junior
Young, Kenneth	Forward	6'2"	175	Sophomore

Prior to the 1969-70 basketball season, principals at three of the city's vocational high schools, which included Mr. Baltimore of Bell, Colonel Posey of Phelps, and the principal of Chamberlain, agreed to purchase a trophy to be awarded to the winner of the basketball games between these three high schools as a recognition of the competition between these schools. The team who defeated the other two teams in a given year would gain possession of the trophy for that year. The first of the three teams to win the trophy for the third time would gain permanent possession of the trophy. The trophy appears in the photo of the 1971-72 Bell Vocats basketball team shown in the collection of photos in this publication.

Throughout the 1971-72 season, the competition was impressive. Through the leadership of our seniors and co-captains, Jesse Smith and Greg Carrington, we were able to put a lot of pressure on the opposition's offensive patterns. Speedsters such as Tibbs, Jordan, Tate, and Harrison were able to cause turnovers by pressuring the ball. Carrington, Tharpe, and Dennis were able to rebound the balls off the backboard behind the opposition's missed shots to start our fast break. The dribbling of Tibbs and the crisp passing of Tibbs and Jordan frequently led to easy baskets for the Vocats.

The season was going well until Carrington, one of our leading players, injured his knee by accidentally walking into a bench in a locker room during the halftime of a game. The injury was so severe that he was unable to continue to play in the game, and Bell came up short and lost, unfortunately. We played two more games with Carrington sidelined by the knee injury. One of those games was against Coolidge, and we lost 82-70. The other was against Roosevelt, and we won 70-44.

Our next scheduled game was against Woodrow Wilson. I had not dressed him to play in the previous two games but after inquiring about how his knee was doing and being told that it was better, I decided to suit him up but not use him during the game. On paper, I thought we were a much better basketball team than Wilson. We were playing them on our home court at Lincoln Junior High School. At halftime we were losing 23-14. We didn't seem to have any energy; we weren't hustling or even shooting well. I knew we needed a spark and I knew Carrington would provide us with one if he were in the game. At halftime after giving my halftime talk, going over the stats, and making a few adjustments, I asked Carrington again how his knee felt. He replied, "Okay." I started him in the second half, and we came from a 13-point deficit to win the game 61-54. Greg Carrington scored 14 of his 17 points in the fourth quarter and was the game's leading scorer. After the game was over, his knee began to swell and became stiff. Consequently, he was unable to play in our last game of the regular season. We had one more game scheduled to play against Roosevelt prior to the Inter-High playoffs. In the game against Roosevelt, we won 70-44 without him. When the Inter-High playoffs began, he was still injured and unable to play. In the first round of the playoffs, we faced the Phelps Tradesmen, a team we had previously beaten earlier in the season. However, we lost to them in the first round, ending our season with a record of 16 wins and 7 losses. Jesse Smith and Greg Carrington made the Inter-High West First Team. Ronald Tibbs made Second Team and Carrington made the All-Metropolitan First Team. Carrington would go on to receive a scholarship to play basketball at Murray State in Kentucky but later transferred to Virginia Union in Richmond, where he made the All-CIAA Basketball Team for two years.

Some of the more talented players I had the pleasure of watching that season were Kenneth Kee, Phelps; Jonathan Smith, Merlin Wilson, and Alonzo "Cheese" Holloway, St. Anthony's; Randolph Campbell, Ballou; Jeffrey Harrison, James Gorham, and James Monroe, McKinley; Cornelius Greene, Dunbar; William Askew and DeCarlo Wiley, Cardozo; Walter Chesley and Larry Arrington, Eastern; William Lynn, Spingarn; Adrian Dantley, Dematha; and Arthur Daniels and Eddie Jordan, Carroll. Cornelius Greene was also an outstanding football player at Dunbar. He received a football scholarship to play for Ohio State. While at Ohio State, he played quarterback and led them to a victory in the Rose Bowl.

At the end of the 1971-72 regular basketball season, I received a long-distance call from Kenny Hudson in Boston. He invited me to bring a team of Washington, DC high school all-stars to Boston to play against comparable teams from New York, Connecticut, and Boston. The event would be the First Annual W.I.L.D. Spring Shootout Basketball Tournament. I was told we could bring ten players and two coaches and all of the expenses would be paid for by the sponsoring company. We were flown roundtrip from Washington National Airport to Boston's Logan Airport. A bus was waiting to pick us up when we arrived, and we were taken directly to Boston University, where the teams were housed in one of the men's dormitories. The games were played in the University's gymnasium. Prior to the beginning of each game, the teams were introduced. The introductions included the name of each team, the name of each player and the high school where he was enrolled, all of his stats, and the honors he had received. Representing the Washington, DC All-Metropolitan team were Gregory Brooks, Merlin Wilson, and Jonathan Smith from St. Anthony's; Adrian Dantley from DeMatha; Randolph Campbell from Ballou; Jesse Smith from Bell; James Monroe from McKinley; Kenneth Kee from Phelps; and Charles "Skip" McDaniels from Carroll.

In the first game, Washington lost a nail-biter to Connecticut by one basket in the last seconds of the game. The next day Washington played New York. Again, prior to the start of the game, the public-address announcer introduced the members of the team and the starting lineup. When he introduced New York's starting lineup, he emphasized that the next player was New York's All-New York City, All-Metropolitan, All-New York State, and All-American, Phil Sellers. The attending crowd gave him a thunderous ovation. When he introduced our team and the starting lineup he began with Adrian Dantley. "From DeMatha High School, standing 6'4" and playing forward. All-Washington Catholic Athletic Conference and All-Metropolitan player, Adrian Dantley." The ovation he received was very sparse, for I am certain few, if any, of the spectators had ever heard of him. After the game got under way, I noticed that Adrian had picked up Sellers and was guarding him man-to-man. I called timeout after five minutes or so to make a few adjustments. As the team gathered around our bench, I said to Dantley, "Adrian, that's great of you to pick up Phil Sellers." And he replied, "I had to because nobody else wanted him."

For the duration of the game, Adrian was like Sellers's shadow when New York had possession of the ball; wherever Sellers went, Adrian was there to play hard-nose defense on him. With about two minutes left in the game and Washington winning by a comfortable margin, I sent in a substitute for Adrian. As he walked off the court and headed toward the bench he received a tremendous ovation from the crowd. They may not have heard of him before this game, but I'm certain they would not forget him after seeing him play. Sellers had scored only 6 points during the entire basketball game. I know most individuals who know Adrian recognize him for his offensive ability and adeptness at scoring or putting the ball in the basket. However, I have seen him accept a challenge head on and come out a winner on the defensive side also. He has a lot of heart and is driven by determination.

Our basketball season had once again come to an end, and we turned our attention to track with the hope that this would be a different year for all of us. When we participated in a dual track meet with other high schools, Bell's trackmen earned a few points in the sprints or dashes and, occasionally, in the relays and field events. However, when all of the DC Public High Schools participated in the Inter-High track meet, Bell was usually not fortunate enough to garner enough first, second, or third-place finishes to have a significant impact on the outcome of the meet. As disappointed as I may have been that year with the outcome of our track season, one rewarding moment was to see one of our young participants develop into a better-than-good athlete because of his individual efforts. His name was Robert Hammond.

When Hammond came out for the track team during his first year at Bell as a tenth grade student, he was notoriously slow. When he attempted to sprint or run as fast as he could, he looked as though he was running in slow motion. I could see he did not have the strength, stamina, endurance, coordination, flexibility, or agility to perform well at the high school level at that point. I could see he was going through a pubescent spurt – a period in which one's body goes through a number of changes and his bony structure outgrows his muscular development. I encouraged him to keep thinking positively and keep doing the conditioning and stretching exercises that we did collectively as a team and assured him good things would happen. He was primarily interested in running the hurdles. I saw him around school and during practice; he seemed to be very shy, bashful, quiet, and not confident in himself. In a few dual meets and the Inter-High relays, Robert was entered in the hurdles but did not fair very well. But with time, things changed for the better. In his senior year, he had grown a few inches and his coordination and strength had improved tremendously. When we participated in the Inter-High relays that year, I entered our team of four in the shuttle hurdles relay. James Nesby ran the first leg, Hammond ran the second leg, Kerry McKinney ran the third leg, and Anthony Phillips ran anchor. It was truly an exciting race, and I took pride in their accomplishment: Bell came in third in that event. Each of them received a medal for their third-place finish, and you knew from their reactions and the expressions on their faces when they accepted their medals just how much it meant to them. They may not have been first-place awards but those medals exemplified far more to them, especially Robert. Nesby, McKinney, and Phillips approached Robert with big smiles to congratulate him on his performance because they realized how much progress he had made since his initial year on the team. After his performance in that meet, I noticed a big change in his demeanor. He seemed to smile more whenever I saw him. He became a more loquacious and self-confident young man; he seemed to have a greater sense of wellbeing about himself.

Other members of the track team had also improved, but no one had improved as much as Robert. At Bell's award banquet, he received a trophy from me for being the "Most Improved" track performer. When he came up to the dais to receive the award, he received a huge ovation from the rest of the athletes and the faculty members in attendance.

Kanns Photo Studio
1966 Bell Vocats Inter-High City Champions football coaching staff from L-R: Ed Allen (asst. coach), Leo Miles (head coach), Julius Edmonson (asst. coach), Billy Coward (asst. coach), and Russell Williams (asst. coach)

Kanns Photo Studio
Bell Vocats Basketball Team 1969-70
Kneeling L-R: L. Holloway, A. Paul, C. Davis, J. Smith, C. Carter.
Standing L-R: R. Hunter, R. Dinkins, K. Barnes, B. Williams, R. Davis, T. Tobias, G. Carrington, Asst. Coach R. Mosby, and Head Coach B. Coward

B. Coward's Collection
DC Inter-High West All-Stars victorious in a benefit basketball game against DC Inter-High East All-Stars in 1970

B. Coward's Collection
1970 Washington Metro All-Stars after winning the Four Cities High School Tournament at the Spectrum in Philadelphia
L-R: Coach Billy Coward (Bell HS), Johnny Lloyd (Anacostia HS), Stanley Washington (Spingarn HS), MVP Eugene Oliver (Fairmont Heights HS), Kermit Ellis (Fairmont Heights HS), Coach McKinley Armstrong (McKinley Tech HS)

Kanns Photo Studio
Bell Vocats Basketball Team 1970-71
Kneeling L-R: J. Cloyd, L. Blake, C. Carr, N. Hall
Standing L-R: R. Dinkins, C. Walker, J. Smith, B. Williams, W. Jordan, C. Wright, T. Tobias, G. Long, G. Carrington, R. Davis, P. London, K. Barnes, L. Battle, R. Hunter, Coach B. Coward
(Asst. Coach R. Mosby not shown)

B. Coward's Collection
The sun reflects on the glass backboard, leaving a glare and making it difficult for Bell players to see the basket at Howard University Burr Gymnasium in 1971. This Inter-High Championship game was won by McKinley.

B. Coward's Collection
Greg Carrington being awarded the Most Valuable Player trophy at the Inter-High Championship game played at Burr Gymnasium, Howard University in 1971

Kanns Photo Studio
Bell Vocats Track Team 1971

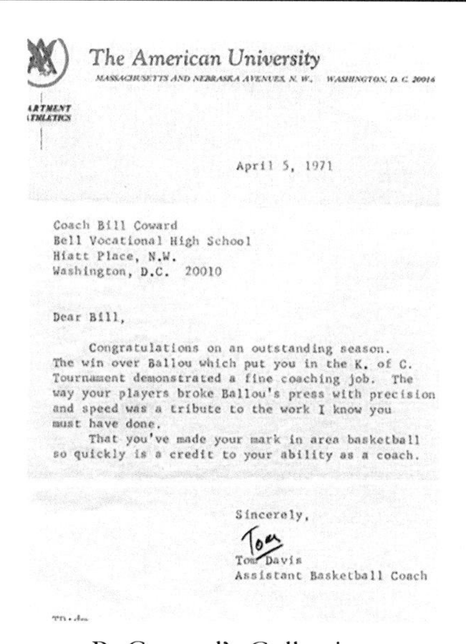

The American University
MASSACHUSETTS AND NEBRASKA AVENUES, N. W., WASHINGTON, D. C. 20016

ARTMENT
ATHLETICS

April 5, 1971

Coach Bill Coward
Bell Vocational High School
Hiatt Place, N.W.
Washington, D.C. 20010

Dear Bill,

Congratulations on an outstanding season. The win over Ballou which put you in the K. of C. Tournament demonstrated a fine coaching job. The way your players broke Ballou's press with precision and speed was a tribute to the work I know you must have done.

That you've made your mark in area basketball so quickly is a credit to your ability as a coach.

Sincerely,

Tom

Tom Davis
Assistant Basketball Coach

B. Coward's Collection

A letter of congratulations from then-American University assistant basketball Coach Tom Davis

Kanns Photo Studio

Bell Vocats Basketball Team 1971-72

Kneeling L-R: D. Battles, H. Harrison, R. Tibbs, B. Whitmyer, J. Smith

Standing first row: L-R: Coach B. Coward, G. Washington, W. Jordan, C. Combs, J. Tate, K. Young (Asst. Coach R. Mosby not shown)

Back row L-R: L. Anderson, C. Wright, G. Carrington, D. Desmond, L. Tharpe

B. Coward's Collection
Gregory Carrington and Coach Billy Coward with individual trophies won by Greg and team trophies won by the Bell Vocats in Greg's three years at Bell 1969-70, 1970-71, 1971-72

Kanns Photo Studio
Bell Vocats Basketball Team 1972-73
Kneeling L-R: R. Davis and D. Plummer
Standing L-R: Asst. Coach W. Cash, G. Chandler, I. McCoy, G. Washington, R. Tibbs, H. Harrison, J. Tate, W. Jordan, C. Wright, L. Anderson, L. Tharpe, Coach B. Coward

Chapter 9

I WAS ENJOYING the challenges of being a high school basketball coach and looked forward to the upcoming 1972-73 season. We had lost some very talented players from the year before but were enthusiastic about the possibilities of the new talent pool. Returning for their senior year were Howard Harrison, Webster Jordan, and Cleo Wright, who formed the nucleus of the team with a very good and talented junior class consisting of Gary Washington, Ronald Tibbs, Larry Tharpe, Leslie Anderson, Desmond Dennis, and John Tate.

The Bell roster for the 1972-73 basketball season was as follows:

Player	Position	Height	Weight	Classification
Anderson, Leslie	Forward	6'4"	185	Junior
Chandler, Gregory	Guard	5'9"	170	Junior
Dennis, Desmond	Forward	6'5"	210	Junior
Harrison, Howard	Guard	5'10"	155	Senior
Jordan, Webster	Guard	6'1"	177	Senior
McCoy, Isaac	Guard	5'10"	158	Sophomore
Tate, John	Guard	6'0"	149	Junior
Tharpe, Larry	Center	6'6"	195	Junior
Tibbs, Ronald	Guard	5'10"	145	Junior
Washington, Gary	Guard	5'11"	180	Junior
Wright, Cleo	Forward	6'4"	170	Senior

Wallace Cash joined the coaching staff as my assistant and Rodger Davis and Durwin Plummer served as managers of the team. During that season we encountered some tough competition. We won our first three games against Chamberlain, Spingarn, and Phelps but lost away-games to Towson Catholic, Atlantic City, and Western. We then won three consecutive games against Ballou, Coolidge, and St. Anthony's along with two losses to Cardozo and Phelps.

The loss to Phelps was particularly hard to digest because we had beaten them in an earlier encounter and were leading them by 15 points at halftime. This game was being scouted by A. B. Williamson, the basketball coach of Eastern High School, our next opponent. Williamson had left at halftime. We seemed to have had control of the game at that point, and he may have surmised we had the game won. I wish this had been the case – in the second half of the game, we couldn't buy a basket. Our players missed easy baskets and Phelps' players made most of theirs. I called timeout on several occasions in an attempt to make adjustments, but nothing seemed to work. Bell ended up losing to Phelps 71-67.

Our next opponent was Eastern at Eastern. This was the first time Bell had a scheduled game at Eastern and the first time I had ever been in Eastern's gymnasium. During the first half of the game, everything was going Eastern's way. Their shots were falling, and there seemed to be a lid on the basket when one of the Vocats attempted a shot. During the second half, the teams switched baskets, but unfortunately for Bell, there was a glare from the sun on our new basket affecting the vision of our players. This situation was reminiscent of the 1970-71 Inter-High Championship game that Bell played – and lost – against McKinley in Burr Gymnasium on the campus of Howard University. The sun had not been a factor when Eastern was shooting at that basket. Eastern won the game 74-62.

After a 63-59 win against Dunbar, Bell played Western for the second time that season and again came up on the short end of things – the score was Western 88, Bell 77. In the three years prior to the 1972-73 basketball season, we had played Western six times and had been fortunate enough to come out with victories each of those six times. Bob Piper, the basketball coach at Western, had not only become the head basketball coach at Western in 1969, the same year in which I became head coach at Bell, but he also lived not too far from me in Northeast Washington. One day prior to the opening of the 1972-73 school year, I was driving by his house and saw him out front with another individual. I stopped to say hello and was told the young man with him was his nephew. Piper had recently traveled to Louisiana, his home state, and brought his nephew back to DC with him with the intent to enroll him in Western for his senior year of high school. His nephew's name was Larry Wright, a name that became well known in the basketball arena in the years to come.

Following the Western game, we came up winners against McKinley, Roosevelt, Woodson, Spingarn, and Wilson. The Wilson game was the last one in the regular season, and the Inter-High playoffs were next on the schedule to determine the Inter-High city champions. Bell was matched up to play Cardozo in the quarter finals. Cardozo had beaten the Vocats in our previous regular season encounter 57-48; however, the Vocats were able to turn the end result around to defeat Cardozo 65-57. Our victory set up another game against Eastern in the semi-finals. Eastern was undefeated in the Inter-High competition with a record of 14 wins and no losses. At halftime Eastern lead 37-33 and continued to lead during much of the second half of the game. Both A.B. Williamson and I were going through a series of decisions to try to out strategize each other. Late in the fourth quarter, Eastern gained possession of the basketball beneath the basket they were defending. As the Eastern players lined up in their formation to take the ball out of bounds, I called a timeout. We were lined up to play Eastern in a zone defense, and I thought they would be in a position to score easily, given Eastern's formation. In order to provide us with a better defense, I told the fellows to switch to a man-to-man formation. Time was called, and when both teams returned to the floor and lined up, A.B. saw we were lined up for a different defense, so he called timeout. I figured he would make an adjustment, so I told my team to switch back to a zone defense. When play resumed, the Vocats stymied Eastern's attempt to make a basket, and we gained possession of the basketball. The ball handling and shooting of Ronnie Tibbs and Webster Jordan brought Bell back to take a 1-point lead, 67-66, with a little less than a minute to play. Eastern tried to play for the last shot, and Johnny Tate stole the ball with very little time on the clock. Webster Jordan made a lay-up as time expired. The final score was Bell 69, Eastern 66. The victory over Eastern put Bell in the finals of the Inter-High playoffs. Western had defeated McKinley Tech 81-68, and in doing so, became our opponents in the championship game.

Western's coach, Bob Piper, had invited a couple of his friends – former Washington Redskins running back Larry Brown and Kansas City Chiefs lineman and professional wrestler Ernie Ladd – to sit on Western's bench to cheer the Raiders on. In the previous two basketball games the two teams had played, Larry Wright was like a thorn in our side. He was an extension of his coach while performing on the court. With his hustle, quickness, desire, determination, and overall constant leadership ability, Larry made it difficult for the Vocats to win each time we played them.

In the championship game Bell came out playing sluggishly early in the first half, and Western got off to a comfortable lead 15-4. Our game plan was to get the ball inside to our big men, Larry Tharpe, Leslie Anderson, or Desmond Dennis. We got only three passes inside to our big men during the first quarter, causing us to fall behind early in the game. In the past years when we played Western, Bell was known to come from behind and win the game on several different occasions; and we did come back in the first half of this game. We came back from a 12-point deficit late in the first half to tie the score at 31. The halftime score was Western 36, Bell 33. Tibbs was very instrumental in bringing us back with his passes and hook shots, along with a full-court press executed by the Vocats. However, it was all Western in the second half. The excellent play of Larry Wright and 6'4" John Smith led Western to run away with the game. The final score was 84-58. Wright had won All-American honors when he played at a high school in his native Louisiana the previous year and made the All-Metropolitan Basketball Team in Washington during the 1972-73 basketball season. Two of Bell's players were recognized for their talents as well: Howard Harrison was selected to the second team and Webster Jordan was selected to the third team in the All-High West Division.

At the conclusion of the 1972-73 basketball season, I received another call from Kenny Hudson inviting me to bring another All-Met basketball team to Boston to participate in the Second Annual W.I.L.D. Spring Shootout. Kenny told me the participating teams would number eight rather than the four in previous years. The teams represented Boston, Atlanta, Chicago, Connecticut, New Jersey, New York, Pittsburgh, and Washington. Each team would be able to bring two coaches and ten players. Arrangements for transportation to and from Boston, as well as eating and housing accommodations on the campus of Boston University, would be taken care of by the sponsors of the tournament. After receiving the invitation to participate in the tournament, I went about the task of holding tryouts for candidates who were interested in representing Washington in the shootout. McKinley Armstrong was again the assistant coach, and we held the tryouts at McKinley High School. More than twenty basketball players came out and participated in the practice sessions. A few days prior to making the cut to ten players, Adrian Dantley approached me and told me he would not be making the trip this time. He told me that college coaches were coming by his house and calling at all hours of the day and night in attempts to recruit him. He had made a decision to go to Notre Dame and would not be going back to Boston. I told him I was sorry that he wasn't going back to Boston with us, but I understood. Shortly after Adrian told me he would not be joining the Washington team that year. Larry Wright, who had been working out with us, informed me that he was leaving that weekend and going back to Louisiana to enroll in Grambling to take classes in summer school. I regretted that he too would not be a part of our team but understood his priorities.

The day before we were scheduled to leave for Boston, Bob Strickland of the Channel 9 television station made a visit to McKinley High School's gym with a camera crew and filmed our last practice. McKinley Armstrong and I had made the roster cuts and posted a list of the ten players who would be making the trip. Those ten players and the high schools they represented were:

Leslie Anderson	Bell Vocational High School
Kenneth Carr	DeMatha Catholic High School
James Gorham	McKinley High School
Larry Herron	Mackin Catholic High School
Alonzo Holloway	St. Anthony's Catholic High School
Eddie Jordan	Carroll Catholic High School
Skip McDaniel	Carroll Catholic High School
DeCarlo Wiley	Cardozo High School
Cleo Wright	Bell Vocational High School
Xavier Yeoman	McKinley High School

After the practice session, Bob Strickland interviewed me and two of the players: Alonzo "Cheese" Holloway and Eddie Jordan. The next day as we were leaving for Boston, the camera crew from Channel 9 met us at National Airport and filmed the team as we boarded the airplane. The video of the interviews and the team boarding the plane was aired later that day on the six o'clock news. This in itself gave us more publicity than our involvement in this tournament had received in the past.

Because eight teams were entered in the single-elimination tournament, it was held over a period of three days rather than two – Friday, Saturday, and Sunday, with the championship game being held on Sunday. When the Washington team arrived on the campus of Boston University, we were assigned to our dormitory rooms before heading for lunch. After lunch we went to the school's gymnasium where the games were being played. The two teams on the floor were Boston, the home team, against the team from Atlanta, Georgia. The Boston team was being coached by former Celtic's player "Satch" Sanders, and all of the Boston players were wearing Celtic-green uniforms. The team from Atlanta fielded a very tall team, led by "Tree" Rawlings at 7' tall. The rest of their starting lineup included players standing 6'10", 6'8", 6'6", and 6'4". We sat in the stands and watched Atlanta beat Boston by 25 points. The Washington team was in the same draw as Atlanta and we were scheduled to play the team from New Jersey. But the team from New Jersey was a no-show, so we got a bye and were scheduled to play Atlanta on Saturday. After the completion of the other games, we went back to the dormitory, where we saw the players and coaches of the night's victorious Atlanta team. One of the coaches from the Atlanta team came up to me and asked, "Are you the coach of the team from DC?" I responded, "Yes." Then he observed that Adrian Dantley was not among our players and asked quizzically, "And you didn't bring Adrian Dantley?" "No," I answered. "Nor did we bring Larry Wright." "Well," he said, "you may as well turn around and go back home. You saw what we did to Boston, didn't you?" I smiled but did not reply.

That evening we had a brief team meeting, and I told the players what the coach from Atlanta had said to me. I emphasized that Atlanta was a very tall team but they weren't as quick or as fast as we were. "We are going to fast-break Atlanta and run those tall fellows out of the gym," I told them. Our tallest players were Kenny Carr and Larry Herron, who were both 6'5", although Larry appeared to be a bit taller because of his Afro hair style.

The next day, just before the game, I again stressed that we wanted to run the fast break at every opportunity. However, realizing the effect this would have on their stamina after a period of time, I cautioned them to let me know when and if any of them got tired while he was in the game to let me know by simply raising his hand and pointing to himself. I would send in a substitute to give him a few moments of rest before returning to the game. I stressed that we wanted to have a good defensive run-and-shoot basketball game. DeCarlo Wiley, Alonzo "Cheese" Holloway, and Eddie Jordan did a very good job of leading our fast break. I think we surprised our opponents – players and coaches alike. We won the game by 15 points. After the game was over and the teams returned to the dormitory, we ran into the coach who had suggested that we turn around and go home rather than play his team. He walked past without saying a word.

By winning the game against Atlanta, we advanced to the championship game against Chicago. With less than four minutes to play in that game, and leading by 5 points, I called a timeout. McKinley and I decided to go into a semi-stall to run time off the clock and take only high-percentage shots, preferably a lay-up. However, our strategy backfired, and we lost the game by 3 points. Nonetheless, we did receive second-place individual trophies and a very nice team trophy for our efforts. Of course, Chicago, having bested us in the championship game, won the first-place trophy and the tournament title that year. Chicago also had two individuals who ultimately played basketball in the NBA. They were Bo Ellis, who played for Marquette on the college level and professionally for the Washington Bullets; and Ricky Green who played for Utah and a few other teams during his NBA career. Connie Hawkins was the coach of the team from Pittsburgh. He had played in the ABA and later with the Phoenix Suns in the NBA and the Harlem Globetrotters.

There were many players of exceptional talent with whom I had the privilege of playing against as the coach at Bell or working with as the coach of the All-Star teams from Washington. As I said, there were many, and I will attempt to remember and name some of them here as well as the schools they attended: Johnny Lloyd, Anacostia; Charles Campbell, Randolph Campbell, William Parker, and Ricardo Cromer, Ballou; Michael Riley, William Askew, Larry Wiley, Michael Flood, and DeCarlo Wiley, Cardozo; Eddie Jordan and Arthur Daniels, Carroll; Glenn Price, Coolidge; Adrian Dantley and Kenny Carr, DeMatha; Keith Byrd and Cornelius Greene, Dunbar; Embee Shaw, Willie Daniels, Walter Chesley, Lovelle Joiner, Larry Arrington, and Tyrone Jones, Eastern; Eugene Oliver and Jerome McDaniels, Fairmont Heights; James Monroe, Lonnie Perrin, Jeffrey Harrison, and James Gorham, McKinley Tech; Kenneth Kee, Phelps; Milton Lundy, Billy Lee, David Lewis, Alonzo Patterson, and Wilbur Thomas, Roosevelt; Stanley Washington, Luther Bethea, William Lynn, and Harry Nickens, Spingarn; Gregory Brooks, Donald Washington, Merlin Wilson, Jonathan Smith, and Alonzo "Cheese" Holloway, Saint Anthony; Victor Kelly, Michael Jenifer, Cornell Robinson, Larry Wright, and John Smith, Western; and Barry Frazier, H.D Woodson.

Eddie Jordan graduated from Archbishop Carroll in 1973 and joined Tom Young at Rutgers in New Brunswick, New Jersey. Tom had been the basketball coach at American University before becoming the head basketball coach at Rutgers. After his playing days were over at Rutgers, Eddie played in the NBA for several years with different teams. He was a member of the Los Angeles Lakers when they won the NBA championship in 1982. He also served as an assistant coach with Rutgers, Old Dominion, Boston College, and the Sacramento Kings. He later became head coach of the Sacramento Kings and the head coach of the Washington Wizards. While he was head coach of the Wizards, his former college basketball coach, Tom Young, became his assistant. Eddie was also subsequently the head coach of the Philadelphia 76ers.

Adrian Dantley graduated from DeMatha and traveled to Notre Dame, where he played basketball for three years prior to his senior year, when he declared hardship and entered the NBA. He was drafted by the Buffalo Braves in 1976. He was traded to the Indiana Pacers and then to the Los Angeles Lakers during the 1977-78 season. In 1979 he was traded to Utah and played with that team for six years. He later played with the Detroit Pistons and then with the Dallas Mavericks in 1988-89. During his fifteen years in the NBA, he received several awards.

Kenny Carr graduated from DeMatha and continued his basketball career at North Carolina State. He played for the Los Angeles Lakers, Cleveland Cavaliers, Detroit Pistons, and Portland Trail Blazers. His NBA career spanned a total of ten years.

Larry Wright graduated from Western High School and enrolled in Grambling State University, where he continued to exhibit his basketball skills. He was drafted by the Washington Bullets and was a teammate of Wes Unseld, Phil Chenier, Bobby Dandridge, and Elvin Hayes when the Bullets won the NBA championship in 1978. After his playing days ended he returned to his alma mater, Grambling, to become the head basketball coach there.

Some of the very capable and skillful coaches I coached against and who presented challenging basketball strategies for me were Herman Daves, Ballou; James Boone, Cardozo; George Leftwich, Carroll; Frank Williams, Coolidge; A.B. Williamson, Eastern; McKinley Armstrong, McKinley Tech; Walter "Rock" Green, Phelps; Dickie Wells, Roosevelt; John Thompson, Saint Anthony's; and John Wood, Spingarn. Admittedly, there were some basketball officials I would have preferred not to have officiating any of my games, but on the other hand there were some very competent officials who refereed our games whom I admired, not only because of their skills and knowledge of the game but also because of their fairness. Among these were Marty Cribbins, Bill Dixon, Lawrence "Larry" Hill, Dr. James "Beannie" Howell, Biff Martin, Richard "Rip" Scott, and Johnny Grier.

During the summer of 1973, I received a telephone call from an individual asking if I would be interested in becoming the basketball coach at Federal City College in Washington, DC. If I were interested, I was told to call Dr. Samuel Barnes, the interim athletic director there. I did call Dr. Barnes, and he told me to submit my resume along with three letters of recommendation to him as soon as possible. Dr. Barnes was the former director of athletics at Howard University. I updated my resume and set out to get the three required letters of recommendation. The first person I talked with was Mr. Charles Baltimore, my former principal at Bell who had hired me and who had been a very successful basketball coach himself at Armstrong High School. I told him I had been contacted about the coaching position at Federal City College and was surprised by his immediate response. "You don't want that job. There are too many problems with that program," he said. I told him that I liked a challenge and would appreciate a letter of recommendation from him. I also contacted Mr. Sylvester "Sal" Hall, the former and very successful teacher, football, and track coach at Cardozo High School. He had also been a successful football coach at Virginia State College and principal at Woodson Junior High School. The third person I contacted for a recommendation was Mr. Joseph "Joe" Coles, the director of the DC Department of Recreation. Incidentally, Mr. Coles was the father-in-law of John Mackey, the former All-Pro tight end for the Baltimore Colts. All three gentlemen complied. The three letters of recommendation along with a positive interview with Dr. Barnes paved the way for a job offer. I got the position with the title of Associate Athletic Director, Basketball and Track Coach at Federal City College. During the same timeframe, Earl Richards, a former well-known football coach at Eastern High School, was hired to become the new football and baseball coach at the College. In fact, we shared the same office in the old Jewish Community Center at 16th and Q streets, Northwest.

Leaving Bell and accepting the position to coach basketball at Federal City left me with mixed emotions because I knew we had the nucleus of a winning basketball team for the 1973-74 season at Bell with the return of players from the previous year. But I had made a decision and would not be coaching that team in another year. Two of the promising young men who had played for me at Bell were Gary Washington and Leslie Anderson.

After graduation from Bell, Gary attended Indian Hills Community College in Centerville, Iowa. While on the basketball team at Indian Hill, Gary made 49 points in one basketball game, establishing a new school record for points made in one game. He left Indian Hills Community College to attend Alderson Broadus College in Philippi, West Virginia. While playing on the Alderson Broaddus basketball team, Gary was the leading scorer in the West Virginia Intercollegiate Athletic Conference (WVIAC), first team All-WVIAC, and honorable mention All-American. Gary graduated from Alderson Broaddus in 1979. I recall Gary visiting me at my home after he had graduated from college. During our conversation, he told me that some of his teammates at Alderson Broaddus often visited him in his dormitory room to ask questions about what to do in certain offensive or defensive situations during a basketball game. As Gary and I talked, he seemed to be citing the same fundamental things I had espoused when we were practicing at Bell, nearly verbatim. This was quite pleasing and a very pleasant surprise to me. Gary's graduation from college and all of the accolades he received while playing basketball at that level were the beginning of his successes. Gary later became the assistant principal of his alma mater, Shaw Junior High School in Washington, DC. He later became the principal at Backus Junior High School and the Choice Academy (formerly Taft Junior High School). In 2009 he was inducted into the Hall of Fame at Alderson Broaddus and I was privileged to be there for the ceremony. He later became the principal of Spingarn Senior High School.

Leslie Anderson played basketball at Bell for two years and attended Laurinburg Institute in Laurinburg, North Carolina, where he played basketball and graduated in 1974. After graduation he received a basketball scholarship to attend George Washington University (GWU) in Washington, DC. He was voted the Most Valuable Player on the basketball team in his junior and senior years in 1977 and 1978. Leslie was drafted in the ninth round of the NBA draft by the Boston Celtics. He was voted into the George Washington University Hall of Fame in 2006, an event I was fortunate enough be invited to attend and to sit at the same table with Leslie and his coach at GWU, Bob Tallent, and his brother, Pat Tallent. Leslie introduced me to Bob and Pat as his high school coach. Bob told me that prior to playing basketball and coaching at GWU, he was on the basketball team at the University of Kentucky when they played Texas Western at Cole Field House on the campus of the University of Maryland in 1966. Also on Kentucky's team was Pat Riley, the former basketball coach of the Los Angeles Lakers, the New York Knicks, and the Miami Heat of the NBA. Kentucky was coached by Adolph Rupp. Bob also said Rupp told him after the game that he could shoot the ball very well but he wouldn't be on the team the following year. But Bob did not tell me why that comment was made. Nonetheless, he transferred to George Washington University after that.

During our conversation at the Hall of Fame celebration, I reminded Bob that shortly after he transferred to GWU several of my friends who had been members of the Kerlips recreational basketball team – Donald Lipscomb, Frank Hart, Harold Dean, Fred "Rabbit" Gaskins, Kermit Banks, and Walt Kennedy – scrimmaged against him and several other fellows in the Tin Tabernacle (the old gym) on the GWU campus. He remembered this occasion, and I can attest to what Adolph Rupp may have observed about Bob: He could definitely shoot.

The schedule for the 1973-74 basketball season had already been finalized before my arrival at Federal City College that year. However, there were a few problems that immediately surfaced. The basketball court in the old community center was not a regulation high school or college-sized court, so we had to find another facility more suitable. Fortunately, we were able to secure Eastern High School's court for practice after their team had completed its daily practices. Federal City paid for the practice time in the gym from 6:00 P.M. until 9:00 P.M. However, Eastern's basketball practice sessions frequently overlapped our starting time. To enable our team to travel from 16th and Q streets, Northwest, to 17th and East Capitol streets, Northeast, we had to lease a bus, which was scheduled to pick up our players by 5:30 P.M. at 16th and Q. Federal City College was spread out across the city in fifteen buildings. Some of the players had late classes and found it difficult to get to the point of departure for practice by 5:30 P.M. Of course, the outcome was there were occasionally not enough players present to enable us to scrimmage. The turnout was between six and seven players. I did not have enough players to make up a ten-player roster and was forced to ask Earl Richards, the football coach, if I could ask some of the members of the football team to come out and play basketball for the school team. He was accommodating and asked his players himself to come out and play basketball. This was good for two reasons: One, they were already eligible academically because they had been cleared to play football; and two, they helped to fill out the basketball roster. Two days prior to our first game, I was as tall as the tallest player on the team at 6' and had only eight eligible players.

We began playing our scheduled basketball games with our home games played mostly at the McKinley Technical High School gym and a few games scheduled at the relatively new H.D. Woodson High School gym. Because we had a scarcity of players on the team and a lack of height, I switched my basketball coaching philosophy from a pressure defense run-and-shoot, or fast-breaking game, to a more conservative zone-defense and control-type offensive game. Unfortunately, we were not a successful team when it came down to wins and losses.

We played Maryland Eastern Shore on their campus. John Bates was the coach there. On Maryland Eastern Shore's team were Billy Gordon, an All-Metropolitan from Richard Montgomery High School in Rockville, Maryland; Joe Pace, a 6'10" center who eventually played for several teams in the NBA, including the Washington Bullets; and Talvin Skinner, who later played in the NBA with the Seattle Supersonics. At that point, the basketball season was, for all intents and purposes, over for the Federal City basketball team. Maryland Eastern Shore defeated us easily and went on to win the NCAA Division II National Championship for the 1973-74 basketball season. Fortunately, we were able to play out the schedule without forfeiting any of the games, but at the end of the season we ended up with only six players and a season record of 2 wins and 19 losses. That was the first time I had ever had a losing season as a basketball coach. This included my experiences coaching my Army company team in Puerto Rico; the post office team when I worked at the main post office located at North Capitol Street and Massachusetts Avenue in DC; Garnet Patterson Junior High School; and Bell Vocational High School. The win-loss record for my four years as head basketball coach at Bell was 62 wins and 29 losses.

One of the first things I did when I became the basketball coach at Federal City College was to join the National Basketball Coaches Association (NBCA). Dr. Barnes suggested I join the NBCA for a number of reasons, one of those being that it would entitle me to purchase a ticket to the Final Four National Championship Games and give me an opportunity to interact with coaches from other schools and divisions. In 1974 the Final Four games were played in the Greensboro Coliseum in Greensboro, North Carolina. As usual, the games were a sellout. The four teams participating in the Final Four that year were UCLA, coached by the "Wizard of Westwood," John Wooden; Marquette, coached by Al McGuire; Kansas, coached by Ted Owens; and North Carolina State, coached by Norm Sloan. North Carolina State, led by David Thompson, the tournament's MVP, won the tournament and became the NCAA National Champion that year. This tournament had significance because it was the first time an African-American had officiated in an NCAA

Final Four. That gentleman was James "Beannie" Howell. Beannie went on to officiate in three more Final Fours in 1975, 1978, and 1982.

Many coaches from the various colleges and universities throughout the country were in attendance at the 1974 Final Four in Greensboro. This, of course, is the norm. Coaches looked to schedule basketball games in upcoming years with other schools not in their conferences. In fact, Don Corbett, the basketball coach of Lincoln University in Jefferson City, Missouri, approached me to ask if I were interested in participating in the Optimist Tournament at Lincoln University on December 27 and 28 of that year. I indicated an interest in participating and assured him I would get back with him for the details later.

Because Federal City's athletic program was going through a building process, Dr. Barnes suggested that I hold a basketball clinic for the area high school coaches and players. This, hopefully, would enable us to open up an opportunity for further interaction with coaches who would perhaps be interested in pursuing a relationship with Federal City College or players themselves who would be interested in pursuing a postsecondary education at the college as a student athlete. I acknowledged that it was a good idea. We were looking for two big-name coaches to invite to headline the clinic. Almost immediately I thought of one of my former instructors at North Carolina College, John McLendon, who was also a well-known former basketball coach at the college. Clarence "Big House" Gaines, the basketball coach at Winston-Salem State College, was another big name who came to mind. We also agreed that other experienced coaches and a skillful and knowledgeable basketball official who could lead a session on rules and regulations might boost the interest of potential participants. Dr. Barnes, as athletic director, contacted Coach McLendon and "Big House" Gaines to invite them to participate as clinicians. I contacted individuals in my own professional circle whose professionalism, expertise, and achievements as coaches I respected and admired. John Thompson was one of these. He had become the head basketball coach at Georgetown the year before (1972) and had been the head basketball coach at Saint Anthony High School. John was asked to be a clinician and agreed to speak on the essentials of a game plan. A.B. Williamson and McKinley Armstrong were also on the top of my list of invitees. A.B. was selected because of his success as a coach at Eastern. His chosen topic for the clinic was "Zone Defense." McKinley was the coach at McKinley Tech and willingly accepted the invitation to talk about "Championship Basketball Beyond the

Gymnasium." James "Beannie" Howell was invited and gave an interpretation of basketball rules and regulations from his perspective as a basketball official. During his presentation, he shared with the audience his experiences as a referee in the NCAA Final Four Championship game in 1974 as well as his many adventures as a tourist in China.

The clinic was held at H.D. Woodson High School in May of 1974. The attendance was modest, but the atmosphere was exciting. There were players and coaches from many of the local high schools in the Washington metropolitan area. I met coaches whom I had not met previously and made contacts I hoped would be advantageous for the FCC basketball program in the future.

Track season was upon us, and I had circulated information about the program hoping to recruit students at FCC interested in participating in track. Those interested were asked to meet with me at the physical education and athletic department building at 16th and Q. We had a sparse turnout; this was not totally unexpected. It was evident that lots of improvisation would be required. FCC did not have a track to work out on, so the few individuals who did show up jogged around the block – to Q Street to 15th to P Street to 16th and back to Q. After jogging, we gathered inside to complete a variety of exercises and a lot of stretching. We then used the harness Exer-Genie to practice starting and to build strong muscles for sprinting and endurance. After completing the conditioning program, we entered a few meets but had little success in winning any of the events. Nonetheless, members of the team gave it their best and were complimented for having done so.

Although it seemed we had just ended our previous basketball season, the 1974-75 season was rapidly approaching. That year I had high hopes that my recruiting efforts for basketball players would not be in vain. During the spring and summer months, I frequented playgrounds all over DC and the nearby Maryland areas talking to players, coaches, and many spectators, trying to get a line on prospective talented basketball players who might be encouraged to attend FCC. Although I did not have any scholarships to offer, no dormitories to house athletes, no dining facilities or meal plans to offer, nor monetary allocations for books, the college could assist these students with financial aid, for those who qualified. Several of the individuals whom I came in contact with had gone to either a junior college or a four-year college away from home but had withdrawn for various reasons after a period of time and returned to the Washington area. We were about the task of having practice with a new sense of vigor for the new basketball season. I had worked hard on getting the fellows in condition and implemented various drills to emphasize various offensive and defensive skills. I was pleased with the outcome during our practice sessions and felt I was successful in getting the effort and performance output from all of the players, with one exception. I recall having a conversation with that individual about what seemed to be a lack of effort in performing the drills. He acknowledged this and promised to improve but continued to display the same attitude and lack of effort throughout the practices. There would be consequences for his behavior.

I wanted all of the players to have a good understanding of all of the rules and regulations of basketball, so I asked Larry Hill and Beannie Howell, two very knowledgeable, competent, and experienced basketball officials, to come to one of our practices. They began with an explanation and demonstration of the rule changes that were made for the upcoming basketball season and then opened up the sessions for questions and answers. After the rules and regulations interpretation, we had an inter-squad scrimmage. With Larry and Beannie refereeing the scrimmage played under a regular game situation, I played all of the players on the team with the exception of the one individual who was not in compliance with my directives in our regular offensive and defensive drills. After the scrimmage, that individual stood up and said, "If you want to play on this team, you do what the coach tells you to do or you won't play. I've learned my lesson."

We finished the previous basketball season with only six players on the roster, and only two of those players returned to play for the 1974-75 season. The starting lineup for that year was comprised of Jeffrey Harrison at point guard, a former All-Metropolitan player at McKinley who had attended Trinidad Junior College in Colorado; Kenny Barnes at shooting guard, who had played for me at Bell and attended Saint Augustine in Raleigh, North Carolina; Leroy Taylor at small forward, who had played at Mackin and then at Niagara University in New York; Larry Tharpe at strong forward, who had played for me at Bell, like Kenny; and Calvin Tuten at center, a former player from Spingarn who had transferred to Federal City from Syracuse University. The Federal City roster for that year was as follows:

Player	Position	Height	Classification	Hometown
Barnes, Kenneth	Guard	6'0"	Junior	Washington, DC
Duvall, Norman	Forward	6'2"	Freshman	Washington, DC
Harrison, Jeffrey	Guard	5'5"	Junior	Washington, DC
Hayes, Stanley	Guard	5'11"	Freshman	Washington, DC
Hicks, Michael	Guard	5'11"	Freshman	Washington, DC
Jordan, Webster	Guard/ Forward	6'1"	Freshman	Washington, DC
Parler, Ronald	Guard	5'10"	Sophomore	Washington, DC
Rodgers, Darryl	Forward	6'2"	Junior	Memphis, TN
Rouse, Ronnie	Guard	5'11"	Freshman	Washington, DC
Smith, Sidney	Forward	6'3"	Freshman	Washington, DC
Swinton, Steven	Guard	5'11"	Freshman	New York, NY.
Taylor, Leroy	Forward	6'4"	Junior	Washington, DC
Tharpe, Larry	Center/ Forward	6'6"	Freshman	Washington, DC
Tuten, Calvin	Center/ Forward	6'6"	Junior	Washington, DC

Our first game of the season was against Hampton Institute. Although we were down at halftime 43-40, we came up winners at the end of the game. The score was 79-70. Jeffrey led all scorers with 24 points, Leroy followed, with 19 and Kenny scored 16 points. We journeyed to Fayetteville State to play the Broncos next. At halftime, the score was 34-33 in favor of Fayetteville. The two teams battled head to head through the second half. Going into the last minute of the game, Fayetteville was leading 78-76 when Kenny Barnes made a basket to tie the score at 78-all. I immediately signaled the players to call a timeout; Kenny signaled and asked the referee for timeout. The referee blew his whistle and signaled timeout for Federal City as a Fayetteville State player was about to throw the basketball inbounds. As our players gathered around me for our next strategy, someone came out of the stands and went directly to the official who had made the call for timeout and talked with him in a very animated and demonstrative manner. After deliberating for a while, the referee approached the scorers' table and signaled a technical foul against Federal City as he verbally announced the call. I immediately asked why and reminded him that we still had another timeout. He responded, "You cannot call a timeout when the other team has possession of the basketball." I told him that we had signaled and asked for a timeout immediately after making the last basket and that he had acknowledged this when he blew his whistle and called timeout for us. It seemed that he made the decision to reverse his call as a result of his conversation with the person who had come out of the stands. Because of this, Fayetteville was awarded a free-throw and then given possession of the ball. The Fayetteville player made the free-throw, giving them a 1-point lead, making the score 79-78 in their favor. They were also awarded possession of the basketball after making the technical foul shot, and the game was over only seconds after they in-bounded the ball.

I surmise that the person who had come out of the stands to converse with the referee was an officials' observer or evaluator. I recognized him as a referee who had officiated a basketball game I had played in when I was in high school. It was in 1949, and I was on the basketball team at Dunbar. We had gone to Fayetteville to participate in a high school basketball tournament on the campus of Fayetteville State. Dunbar was playing a team from Elizabethtown, NC. In those days, we played with two referees, one usually positioned at the baseline beneath the basket on the left sideline and the other usually in the vicinity of the half-court line. At one point during the game, I recovered a loose ball near the baseline, and the referee near the half-court line blew his whistle and called me out-of-bounds. I was standing two feet inside the baseline when I gained possession of the basketball. The other referee was in position on the baseline and could clearly see that I was inbounds because he did not call me out-of-bounds, nor did he signal me out-of-bounds by blowing his whistle. I explained to the referee at half-court that the other official didn't call me out-of-bounds and seemed to be in a position to see if I were either inbounds or out-of-bounds. The official at half-court, the one who had indicated that I was out-of-bounds when I recovered possession of the ball, called for the ball and gave possession of the ball to Elizabethtown. We lost that game also. It was ironic: The same individual who had come out of the stands onto the court during the game in 1974, when I was coaching a game between Federal City and Fayetteville State, to talk with the referee about a call was the same person who, in his role as a referee, had called me out-of-bounds in 1949 during a high school basketball tournament between Dunbar and Elizabethtown. After twenty-five years, could this have been just a coincidence?

Prior to the start of the 1974-75 season, I contacted Don Corbett to commit to participating in the Optimist Basketball tournament at Lincoln University. After following the procedural steps necessary for such a trip, the Federal City team and coaching staff flew out to Jefferson City for the tournament. It was a nice experience, but we came up a bit short on the score.

Throughout the basketball season, I saw leadership qualities surfacing from two players who had played for me at Bell. They were Kenny Barnes and Larry Tharpe. Kenny was exemplified by his continuous hustle, determination, and never-say-die attitude. Larry constantly shouted out words of encouragement to his teammates in the locker room and on the basketball court, particularly when one of his teammates made a mistake. You could hear Larry's voice in the background saying, "That's okay," as he called to his fellow player by name. "Let's make up for it the next time. Just keep hustling. You'll make some mistakes during the game, but you'll make up for those mistakes through hustle and determination."

Kenny was usually the second leading scorer on the team and one of the leaders on defense, leading to steals against the opposition. Along with Jeffrey Harrison, he ignited our fast break. Larry was one of the better shot-blockers on the team, and he, Calvin Tuten, and Leroy Taylor were the leaders in rebounding, leading to the outlet passes to start our fast break.

But we had our work cut out for us when we played Coppin State. Coppin State was led by Coach John Bates. Bates was the head basketball coach at Maryland Eastern Shore during the 1973-74 basketball season and led them to the NCAA Division II National Championship that year. From that championship team, he brought to Coppin State his center, Joe Pace who was 6'10". Pace was averaging 25 points per game. Prior to the game with Coppin State, part of my game plan against him was for our players to drive to the basket directly toward Joe in an attempt to get him in foul trouble early. The Panthers left the dressing room to warm up on the court after I had given them our strategy. I followed them to the court after ten minutes or so and was told almost immediately by one of our team managers that Federal City had been assessed a technical foul. When I asked the reason for the foul, I was told that he didn't know. I asked which official had made the call, and he pointed him out. I approached the official and asked if he had called a technical against my team and, if so, why. He stood there with his arms folded, looking at the teams warm up, but he did not respond. I asked again why a technical foul had been called against us, and again he did not reply. Then I said, "You know that I am the coach of the Federal City team, and I have a right to know the reason for the technical foul." But he still did not answer. After making a third attempt to get a response, he finally said, "For dunking the basketball." He did not look at me as he responded but continued to stand near half-court with his arms folded, rocking back and forth on his heels. In retrospect, he seemed to reflect a rather pompous attitude, even before the game got underway.

During the 1974-75 basketball season, dunking the ball in the basket was a violation of the rules and regulations. If this took place during warm-ups or during the game, the violating team was assessed a technical foul. I knew this and our players knew that because they had been told this prior to the start of the season by Larry Hill and Beannie Howell, the two officials who had refereed one of our scrimmages before we began our regular basketball schedule that year. I found out which player was guilty of the infraction and asked why he had done that. He acknowledged that he was guilty and simply shrugged it off. I reprimanded him and cautioned him against doing it again and reminded him that all of us had to remember the rules – coaches and players alike.

The game plan I had devised for our match-up against Coppin was working in the first half, as our players took the basketball to the paint (the three-second area) and drove toward the basket in attempts to get Joe Pace into foul trouble. We succeeded in getting him to commit three fouls early. As a result, Coppin's coach had to pull his center out relatively early in the first half. We were leading at halftime with the score at 58-53. During the first half, the official who had called the technical fouls against us during the warm-up called several more technical fouls against both teams during the game. In the second half of the game, we had possession of the ball, and Jeffrey was dribbling down the court when he was slapped on the hand by a Coppin player. Jeffrey called the slap on the hand – which had been loud enough to have been heard throughout the gym – to the attention of the official, but nothing was said or done. I protested to the official, and he called a technical foul against me. Later on in the game, a similar situation surfaced with about five minutes left in the game. Again, Jeffrey was slapped on his hand as he was dribbling down the court and again he called the incident to the attention of the same official. It was incredulous that he called a technical foul on Jeffrey. At that point, I confronted him and said, "On two occasions one of Coppin's players fouled Jeffrey Harrison and nothing was done about it. Why didn't you call the fouls that were obvious?" Suffice it to say, he immediately called a technical foul on me. I pursued the question, nonetheless, and he replied, "If you don't shut up and sit down, I'm going to throw you out of the game." My response was, "As badly as you are officiating, you may as well do that." He blew his whistle, signaled a technical, and pointed to the door. This was the first time in my coaching career that I had a technical foul called against me for any reason during a basketball game, let alone being asked to leave the court. That one official called a total of ten technical fouls in that one game.

Given all the drama going on, our players were doing a good job in executing the game plan, particularly against Pace. He scored only 10 points – 15 points below his average. Harrison scored 27 points, and Leroy Taylor scored 20 points for the Panthers in a losing effort. The final score was Coppin State 98, Federal City 94. The good news is that the offensive referee who officiated in that game did not referee in any more games for Federal City College during my tenure.

As the tail end of our schedule progressed, we began to lose some of the players who were getting a significant amount of playing time and played a vital role in the success we had earlier in the season. Personal problems surfaced, resulting in missed practices and games. Several of the players told me that they were getting only half the financial aid money they qualified for, further exacerbating their other problems. We finished the season with 10 wins and 11 losses. Before the season had begun, I was hopeful of finishing with a recorded average of .500 or better. Unfortunately, because of circumstances and lack of luck, we came up one game short of our goal. However, there was some good news. Jeffrey Harrison, our 5'5" guard, was the 31st leading scorer in the nation according to the National Collegiate Sports Service citing the official basketball statistics for the final NCAA Division II scoring. Through 21 games he had a scoring average of 21.1 points per game. His scoring average made him the leading point-getter of all the colleges and universities in the Washington metropolitan area. That included American University, Georgetown, Howard, George Washington, and Maryland. Jeffrey was the individual whom I had kept out of the scrimmage because he was not following instructions during our drills and practices prior to our first game of the season.

Gurley Photo
Federal City College Basketball Team 1973-74

Gurley Photo
Coach Billy Coward explains a strategy to Ric Jameson as other Federal City College players and Asst. Coach Richard Mosby listen in 1973-74

Gurley Photo
Federal City College Basketball Team 1974-75
L-R: Mgr. Johnny King, Jeff Harrison, Ron Parler, Mike Hicks, Stanley Hayes, player name unavailable, Steve Swinton, Kenneth Barnes, Webster Jordan, Darryl Rodgers, Norman Duval, Sidney Smith, LeRoy Taylor, Larry Tharpe, Calven Tuten, manager, Asst. Coach Richard Mosby, Coach Billy Coward

Gurley Photo
Federal City College players listen to Coach Coward during a game, L-R: Sidney Smith, Leroy Taylor, Calvin Tuten, Coach Coward, Asst. Coach Richard Mosby, and Kenny Barnes during the 1974-75 basketball season

The Washington Post SPORTS

...R1

SATURDAY, FE

By Gerald Martineau—The Washington Post

Courtesy of *The Washington Post*
Federal City College Coach Billy Coward emphasizes a point to team leading scorer Jeffrey Harrison in 1975

Chapter 10

DURING THE SPRING of 1973, my wife, Tamara, and I became interested in tennis. Several of our friends were already involved in the sport and encouraged us to begin playing as well. We went to the courts at 3rd and Van Buren in Northwest Washington – better known as Takoma Park by the locals – to practice hitting against the wall as a first step at learning how to control the ball. Years before we became interested in tennis, we had tried to encourage our daughters to play tennis because of the convenience of the courts and our desire to expose them to another activity – we lived across the street from the courts. We bought them new racquets and took them to the courts on several occasions, but they seemed to be more interested in ballet and swimming than tennis. So, we let them pursue their own individual interests. Nonetheless, we hung on to the racquets over the years and used those same racquets when we began to play tennis. When we began, we were far from ready to venture out into the real world of tennis, but we practiced against the wall, then tried hitting back and forth over the net as we attempted to learn to control the ball; concentrate on our footwork; and perfect our strokes. We eventually got up enough nerve to play mixed-doubles or doubles against two men, if there were no other women on the court, and occasionally won. At this point, we decided it was time to purchase new tennis racquets more suited to our individual skill levels and style of play.

That same year, we were invited by friends of ours, Donald and Johnella Lipscomb, whom I had known most of my life, to a tennis party at the Whitemarsh tennis facility in Bowie, Maryland. After that we were hooked. We were encouraged by the Lipscombs, who had become members of the club, to join and become part of a mixed-doubles league playing there on Friday nights. Another advantage in joining was that we would also be able to take lessons from the club's teaching pro. After taking a few lessons from Lutz, the teaching pro, we joined the Friday night mixed-doubles league. After playing several matches, our tennis skills showed some improvement, and we began to play much better as a team. There were usually ten or eleven teams competing in each session, lasting throughout the indoor season. As we played and became more confident, we gradually moved up in the standings and finished that year in third place, the next year in second, and ultimately finished in first place on three separate occasions. The league became very competitive and was composed of mostly husbands and wives. Trophies were awarded to the first-, second-, and third-place finishers. Other individuals whom we had met at Takoma Park – Lois and Charles Coleman, and Henry Kennedy, Sr. and his daughter, Angela – also played in that league, though at a higher level.

Over the years, there had been many individuals who were excellent tennis players with whom I was acquainted either in high school, the neighborhood, or in other circles in Washington. I enjoyed watching them play but did not have much of an interest in taking up the sport until then. Some of the names may be recognizable to many readers of this book who grew up in Washington: Clyde, Tommy, and Harold Freeman, Riddick Vann, Benjamin Metz, Paul Alexander, and William Cornet Pryor. Through the years most of these individuals participated in the local tennis tournaments, such as the DC Open, the DC Closed, the Shiloh Tournament, the Turkeys Tournament, the Mall Tournament, and the Kennedy Tournament. Many of these individuals went on to become well known in their chosen professions. Clyde Freeman finished the Howard University School of Medicine and became a gynecologist. His youngest brother, Harold, also finished medical school and became the chief of surgery at Harlem Hospital in New York City. William Cornet Pryor became a judge in the Court of Appeals in the District of Columbia.

Norma Holloway and Julius "Jay" Johnson, who later became her husband, occasionally played mixed-doubles with us at the East Potomac tennis facility. Both Norma, known professionally as Norma Holloway Johnson, and Jay later became judges in Washington; she was also the first African-American female to become a Chief Judge in the US District Court. Although my brother, Jerry, did not play tennis, he was a successful tennis coach at Phelps Vocational High School, winning three Eastern Division titles in the DC Inter-High League in the 1960s.

Mr. Willis S. Thomas, Sr., a gentleman who taught me when I was a student at Garnet Patterson Junior High, was the tournament director for the DC Open, the Mall, DC Closed, and, on occasion, the American Tennis Association's (ATA) national tournament. Those tournaments were held at the Banneker, Turkey Thicket, and Catholic University tennis facilities. His son Willis S. Thomas, Jr. and Arthur Ashe won the junior doubles championships at the ATA national championship tournament during the mid-1950s. The American Tennis Association is, incidentally, the oldest African-American sports organization in the United States. It was formed in Baltimore, Maryland, in 1916. Willis Thomas, Jr., who enjoyed the sport as well and was very active in the ATA, later coached such players as Zina Garrison, Katrina Adams, Lori McNeil, and Rodney Harmon, among others who became professional, and in some cases, ranked players. He also recently served as president of the American Tennis Association, Inc.

Then there was the Henry Kennedy family. Henry Kennedy, Sr. was the patriarch of the family, an avid tennis player, and a devout fan of the sport. He held a tennis tournament named for him at the Takoma Park tennis courts for years. The courts at 3rd and Van Buren were named in his honor – the Henry H. Kennedy Memorial Tennis Courts – after his death several years ago. His two sons, Henry, Jr. and Randall, were very good tennis players, each winning a number of tournaments over the years. Henry, Jr. became a federal judge in the District of Columbia, and his brother, Randy, as he was known, earned a law degree and became a professor of law at Harvard. The youngest sibling in the family, Angela, went to Princeton in New Jersey and was the roommate of the current First Lady of the United States of America, Michelle Obama.

There have been other tennis players – some well-known, others not as well-known – who have had some connection with individuals whom I have known or have been related to. One of these was Althea Gibson, who became the first African-American female to win the Wimbledon singles championship in 1957 and again in 1958. She won the US Open singles championship in 1957 and 1958 as well. Although she was born in South Carolina and lived in New York City in Harlem at an early age, she lived in Wilmington, NC, as a teenager and attended Williston High School. One of her early tennis mentors was Dr. Hubert Eaton, who had a tennis court at his home in Wilmington where Althea often played. While enrolled at Williston, she was taught by a cousin of mine, Sarah Avant Moultrie. Sarah's father, Dr. Frank W. Avant, and his brother, Dr. W. George Avant, my grandfather, were players on Howard

University's first football team in 1893, as mentioned earlier. Sarah's husband, H. Carl Moultrie, I, was a longtime executive secretary for the Omega Psi Phi fraternity and later became a very respected individual in the judicial field as the Superior Court Chief Judge in Washington, DC. Shortly after his death, the Superior Courthouse building at 500 Indiana Avenue, Northwest, in Washington was renamed the H. Carl Moultrie, I Courthouse in his honor.

After Althea's graduation from high school, she attended college at Florida A&M in Tallahassee. Also attending Florida A&M was fellow student Ernest Fears, who became a well-known sports figure in his own right. Ernie, as he was known, became a very successful basketball coach at Norfolk State College in Norfolk, VA. In 1969, Norfolk State won the CIAA Basketball Tournament held in Greensboro, NC, an event my wife and I witnessed. On that championship team was Bobby Dandridge, who went on to the NBA and played on NBA championship teams with the Milwaukee Bucks and the Washington Bullets in 1978. Both Ernie and Bobby were avid tennis players as well. Both have participated in various tennis tournaments throughout the Washington, DC area.

Another outstanding tennis player in the DC area was local legend Edgar Lee. Edgar attended Virginia Union University and Howard University in the mid-1930s. He was ranked 4th in the Mid-Atlantic Lawn Tennis Association (MALTA) in men's singles in 1944. In 1982 he was ranked 8th in the men's top 70 singles by the United States Tennis Association (USTA). Edgar also won men's 45 singles titles in 1957-1962, 1965, and 1969 in the ATA.

Dr. Robert W. Johnson, a dentist from Lynchburg, Virginia, and tennis coach, was very instrumental in helping shape the tennis careers of both Althea Gibson and Arthur Ashe. Arthur went on to win the Junior National Tennis Championship in 1960 and 1961. He received a scholarship to play tennis at UCLA in 1968. After turning pro, he won several majors in his career: the US Open men's singles title in 1970; the Australian Open men's singles title that same year; and the men's singles title in 1975, beating Jimmy Connors in the championship matches at Wimbledon. Dr. Johnson's son, Bobby, attended North Carolina College when my brother was there and later when I was a student there as well. He became the tennis coach at McKinley Tech in the DC Public Schools and later coached the tennis team at Howard University. One of Bobby's former players at Howard was Mike Okala, whom I saw for the first time in a tournament in 1973 at the tennis stadium at 16th and Kennedy. I was impressed with his precise strokes and quiet but determined demeanor as he moved about the court. I enjoyed watching him play and remember thinking, as I am certain that many others have at one time or another, that I wish I could play as well as he. Mike won that match. I found out afterward that he was from Harlem. From that day forward, he became a very active player in tournaments in the area and later coached several local league teams. Bobby also had three sons, Bobby, Jr., Julian, and Lange, who became very good tennis players in their own right.

Another tennis player who was born in New York City but came to Washington in 1949 to pursue a degree in higher education at Howard University was Norman "Norm" Fitz. I did not know him at that time but got to know him as I became more involved in the sport myself. I later learned that one of Norm's cousins, Althea, had been married to my uncle, Dr. Frank Avant, my mother's brother, who lived in Rocky Mount, NC. Norm began playing tennis at some point after graduating from college and has had a long relationship with various aspects of the sport as a player, official, and administrator. During the era of segregated country clubs in this area, Norm was one of the first African-Americans to play in these clubs. He was soon ranked in the top ten in the Middle Atlantic Lawn Tennis Association (MALTA). Since that time, he has been ranked as number one, two, or three in every senior age group in which he has played in MALTA or the Greater Washington Tennis Association (GWTA). Norm has also competed in national tournaments as a senior player and has been ranked among the top twenty players in the country. He has officiated in several US Open tournaments in New York; in the old Washington Star Tournament held at 16th and Kennedy; as well as in other tournaments in the Washington Metropolitan area and other parts of the country. When Arthur Ashe participated in tournaments in the city, he stayed with Norm and his family.

There were any number of very good tennis players in the area who could be seen frequently in local tournaments. Some who come to mind were Phil Lucas, Olin Dupree, Isom "Ike" Upkins, and John Osaka. I don't recall seeing Calvin Snowden on the courts at that time, but I do recall seeing him on the football field at Roosevelt High School. When he graduated from high school, he received a football scholarship to attend Indiana University and from there played professional football in the NFL for the San Diego Chargers. He may not have played tennis before, but today he is an avid tennis player. He is among many others who have acquired a passion for tennis after playing other sports as younger men or women.

In 1983 I was privileged to have had the opportunity to participate in a sports celebrity tennis tournament held at 16th and Kennedy. I did not consider myself to be a celebrity then or now, but I was honored to be asked to join a select group of people who were celebrities in their own right in various professional sports, entertainment, television, radio, or business. It was a doubles tournament, and each of the celebrities was paired with a lesser known individual. I was paired with Sam Jones, a former member of the Boston Celtics. Sam and I had attended the same college in North Carolina in the 1950s but had never played tennis together before then. He played basketball in college and I played football. Other celebrities in that particular tournament were Glenn Brenner, sportscaster for Channel 9; Bill Martin, vice president of Riggs Bank; Bessie Stockard, coach of the women's varsity basketball team at Federal City College; Harold Bell, sportscaster for radio station WINX; Timmy Newsome, former running back at Winston-Salem State University and the Dallas Cowboys; and Jim "Bad News" Barnes, a former NBA player.

The format for the tournament was single elimination: If a team lost their first match, they were eliminated from further competition. The first doubles team to win six games advanced. Sam and I were fortunate to continue to win a total of five straight matches against five other teams. We encountered Bill Martin and his partner; Harold Bell and his partner; Bessie Stockard and her partner, David Merriweather; and two other doubles teams whose names I cannot recall. After our fifth straight win, which led us to the championship match, we played Bad News Barnes and his partner. After a very competitive match, Sam and I came out victorious, and each of us won a beautiful doubles championship trophy. Of course, our opponents received the runner-up trophy.

There were other celebrities in attendance who did not participate but were well known in the area. One was Ken Beatrice, the radio sportscaster whose opening line on his show was "You're next on Sports Call." Another was the former basketball player with the 1978 NBA champion Washington Bullets and current color commentator on TV for the Washington Wizards Phil Chenier.

Bill Martin's daughter, Stacey, was an up-and-coming tennis player at the time. Bessie was not only an outstanding basketball coach but an outstanding tennis player as well. She has won a women's singles title in one of the ATA championship tournaments. Bad News Barnes attended Texas Western (currently the University of Texas at El Paso). He played on the US Olympic basketball team in Japan in 1964, winning the gold medal in the process. He was a number-one draft choice of the New York Knicks and also played with the

Baltimore Bullets, LA Lakers, Chicago Bulls, and the Boston Celtics. He retired from the NBA and as an entrepreneur created, produced, and marketed a barbeque sauce that bore his name: Bad News.

The following year, the celebrity tennis tournament was held again. Playing that year was Donnie Simpson, the radio disc jockey for radio station KYS; Kathy Blount, who was with WTTG TV and then with Channel 20 on "Newsprobe," which she produced and hosted; and Johnny Sample, a former football player with the University of Maryland Eastern Shore, the New York Jets, and the Washington Redskins. He was also an official at the US Open and served as a lines person and chair umpire at several of the Open matches through the years. Johnny and his partner won the tournament that year.

During the 1989-90 indoor season, I was invited to play tennis with a group on Thursdays from 8:00 to 10:00 P.M. in the bubble at the same facility. Conrad Williams coordinated the group and invited Douglas "Doug" Vincent and Kenneth "Ken" Mundy to complete the foursome, in addition to myself. On Thursday, January 18, 1990, we had concluded a pleasant two hours of tennis and friendly conversation between games and headed home. When I reached my home shortly afterward, I turned on the TV to listen to the ten o'clock news on Channel 5 and heard that Mayor Marion Berry had been detained at the Vista Hotel. I immediately changed channels to see if I could catch the eleven o'clock news on Channel 4 and saw Ken Mundy, still in his tennis attire, conversing with Marion Berry in Berry's kitchen. Apparently a camera crew had rushed to the mayor's house in Southeast Washington to film the event. As I watched and listened more closely, I told my wife that I had just finished playing tennis with Ken. I did not know until then that he was Berry's lawyer. The following Thursday when I returned to the bubble for our weekly tennis time, I told Ken what I had seen on TV the week before. I asked how he had gotten to Berry's house so quickly that night and was told that he lived in Kensington and had gone straight home. When he arrived, the light was on the porch, the front door was open, and his wife was waiting for him. She told him the mayor wanted him to come to his house as soon as possible and was sending a car to pick him up. The rest of the story has been well documented.

In 1984 Tamara and I became members at the Aspen Hill Club. "Tam" joined a group of ladies who played tennis for a period of two hours on Saturdays during the indoor season, and I got together with a group of fellows to play on Sunday mornings from nine o'clock until eleven o'clock. We occupied two courts because we usually had twelve or thirteen individuals in the group; eight of these were scheduled to play on a rotating basis on any given Sunday. We did this every Sunday from September through April each year from the late 1980s through the 2005 indoor season. Among those who participated were Al Baker, Bill Bush, Cameron Byrd, Jeff Caplan, Art Cohen, Al Der, Rawlin Donald, Mark Green, Earl Hunt, Paul Joyner, Akira Kondo, Darrell Lipscomb, Herb Ritter, Charlie Teller, Gordon Mickelson, Phil Nicholson, and Sam Werner. Preceding our group onto the court during those years were two gentlemen who had been playing singles on a regular basis. One was Isiah "Ike" Leggett and the other was Sol Graham. Ike was a teacher at the Howard University School of Law. He was also a former assistant dean of the law school. As of this writing, he is the Montgomery County Executive in the State of Maryland. I would see both of them at the Aspen Hill Club occasionally. The Aspen Hill Club was as much a social environment as a sports environment. I ran into Jay Johnson, an avid fitness buff, there almost on a weekly basis. Jay not only worked out in the fitness center but swam and played tennis as well. When we found a moment or two to sit in the lounge, we had some great conversations about a variety of topics.

A few years later, before I sustained a shoulder injury, I joined a group of older men who formed a senior team to represent the Aspen Hill Club against other senior teams in Montgomery, Howard, and Baltimore counties. Our senior team was captained by Arthur Cohen. The requirements for the senior league were that each player had to be at least fifty years of age and a current USTA member. We played each team on an "alternating home" basis – we played each team once on our home courts at Aspen Hill and then on their home court at their respective home facility. Some of the opposing senior teams were from Indian Springs, Edgemoor, and Kenwood.

During the 1996-97 fall and winter indoor tennis season, a few of my tennis friends got together to play men's doubles at the Fairland tennis facility in Laurel. Those individuals were Tom Hammond, "Noonie" Millard, and Bill Vault. I had reserved courts for the season on Wednesdays for two hours each. Bad News Barnes filled in for any of us who may have needed a substitute. It became very competitive when Noonie and Bill Vault were on the court as a doubles team against Tom and me. Incidentally, Tom's sister, Alexis Roberson, was the director of the DC Recreation Department, at the time.

Throughout the years, my wife and I have attended the CIAA basketball tournaments wherever they may have been held – in DC, Durham, Greensboro,

Hampton, Norfolk, Richmond, Charlotte, and Winston-Salem. In 1998 the tournament was held in Winston-Salem. During the same week as the basketball tournament in Winston-Salem that year, an indoor tennis tournament was also being held nearby for all interested tennis players who were attending the CIAA tournament, coordinated by David Lash, a local tennis professional. Tamara and I entered the tournament as the only mixed doubles team; all of the other teams were all male. Our first and only match in the tournament was against Earl "The Pearl" Monroe and his business and doubles partner, Kendall Flowers. Earl had undergone hip replacement surgery several months prior to the tournament, but this did not seem to hinder his tennis game. He seemed to be just as assertive and aggressive on the tennis court as he had been on the basketball court. He and Kendall won the match in two straight sets – 6-2, 6-3. Nonetheless, it was a fun match, and Tamara and I thought we had held our own under the circumstances despite the score. We had, after all, won five games against two very tough opponents. Lash, the coordinator and tournament director, had also been Tamara's high-school basketball coach when she played on the girls' basketball team at Carver High School in Winston-Salem.

When Tamara retired in 2000, she began playing tennis several times a week on Tuesday, Thursday, and Saturday mornings during the fall and winter seasons with different groups at Aspen Hill. While she was on the tennis court, I took that opportunity to workout in the fitness center, usually for an hour and forty-five minutes to two hours. Even before retirement, she played regularly on Saturday mornings and occasionally on Tuesday or Thursday evenings. She not only played several times a week but became interested in playing USTA league tennis as well and joined several teams over the course of many years. The captain of one of those teams was Nancy O'Neill, the wife of Geoff O'Neill, one of the teaching pros at Aspen Hill. They began playing in the USTA Adult League and entered the Senior League as they got older. Nancy's teams were successful at each level, advancing to Sectionals on many occasions and advancing to Nationals in San Diego in 2000. The majority of the ladies on Nancy's teams had played together for a number of years and seemed to enjoy the compatibility and goodwill that existed among members of the group; they found opportunities to socialize off the courts as well as on the courts at house gatherings and occasional lunches. Even today, a few of them still get together once in awhile for lunch. And, yes, most of them are still playing tennis.

Throughout my years of employment I have been fortunate enough to have had jobs that were involved in some way with sports. In 1981 I became an administrator of recreational activities for students, faculty, and staff at Howard University. My office was in the Armour J. Blackburn Center, Student Union Building. On the lower level of the building was the recreation center with an eight-lane bowling alley, pool tables, ping-pong tables, foosball tables, video games, and game rooms for board and card games. Most of the activities were competitive team events ending in tournament play. Trophies were awarded to the first-, second-, and third-place winners in each event, who then represented Howard at the Annual Association of College Unions International (ACUI) tournament. Howard was a member of the Mid-Eastern Section of the ACUI. Other college and university members were from Delaware, Pennsylvania, Virginia, West Virginia, Maryland, and the District of Columbia. Some of the sites for the regional tournaments were at West Virginia University, Penn State University, and the University of Maryland. The winners competed at the National ACUI Tournament.

Howard's men's and women's bowling teams competed against other bowling teams and were members of the ACUI on a team-versus-team basis until the regional tournament was held.

The intramural sports and weight training program were held in the Burr Gymnasium and Greene Stadium. Soccer matches were played in the lower gymnasium, as were the basketball games. Flag football was played in Greene Stadium. Leagues were formed and a round-robin schedule was made up for all the participating teams. Glenn Harris was the coordinator for the intramural program from 1977 to 1985. Prior to becoming the intramural coordinator, Glenn was a Howard University student and a catcher on the baseball team from 1970 to 1974, and a very good catcher, I might add. His coach was Chuck Hinton, the former Major Leaguer who played outfield for the old Washington Senators. A teammate of Glenn's during those years was Eugene "Rock" Newman. Rock played third base for the Bison and later became internationally famous for being the manager and guiding the career of former heavyweight boxing champion Riddick Bowe. Glenn was also a former public-address announcer for the Howard University basketball team's home games in Burr Gymnasium. He later became a sports commentator for the University's radio station WHUR. Glenn moved into the television world by being a sports commentator on Channel 8 in the DC area and continues to work in that capacity today. Gus Johnson also played baseball when he was a student at Howard University in the early 1990s and served as an intern with Glenn on WHUR. He later became a sportscaster locally on WTTG Channel 5 in Washington and later nationally on CBS.

Charlie Neal, an occasional sports commentator for WRC/NBC television Channel 4, helped to referee the intramural basketball games. He was also a sportscaster for many of Howard's football and basketball games as well as other historical black college football and basketball games over Black Entertainment Television (BET) and more recently for ESPN.

At the end of my work day, I enjoyed the opportunity to run and jog in Greene Stadium several times each week. For years I have made an attempt to work on staying in good physical condition, and working at Howard afforded me the opportunity to do this more frequently. In the late 1980s, there was a tight end on the football team coached by Willie Jeffries named Jimmy Johnson. Jimmy was usually out running and exercising by himself when I arrived on the track. We often ran some 200- and 300-yard sprints together. I tried to encourage him to continue to work hard if he wanted to play football at the next level. He did eventually play in the NFL for several teams, including the Washington Redskins and is currently an assistant coach with the Minnesota Vikings.

A few years later in 1992-93, Alfred "Butch" Beard became the basketball coach at Howard. He had played on the Louisville University basketball team with Wes Unseld and also on the Seattle Supersonics basketball team in the NBA. The Sonics beat the Washington Bullets in the 1979 NBA championship game. Butch eventually became a regular on the track at Greene Stadium, and I frequently joined him in our routine jogs. At one point I began running 220, 330, and 440 yards. One day, without explanation, Butch said he was going to jog outside the stadium and took off. Butch's assistant basketball coach, Jerry Eaves, also a former Louisville and NBA player, came out to jog with us one day. On that particular day, I was running 440 yards four times. I ran one and walked one. I had run two 440s and was finishing my walk-around after my second 440 run when Jerry asked me what I was getting ready to do next. I told him I was about to run a half-speed quarter. I started running, and when I got to a spot about ten yards from where I started, Jerry caught up with me and said, "Great day in the morning, Mr. Coward. How old are you?" I told him that I would be sixty-one in October. Jerry seemed surprised that at sixty-one I could still run the quarter and called to Butch in amazement, "Butch." Butch, who was nearby and had heard the conversation, responded, "I told you not to mess with the man." I told Jerry if I had known he was running behind me and trying to catch me, I would have turned it up a notch. He smiled. Butch Beard left Howard after coaching the basketball team to a MEAC championship. He became the head coach of the New Jersey Nets of the NBA, and

Jerry went along as his assistant basketball coach. Jerry later became the head basketball coach at North Carolina A&T and has been there for several years. On another day when I was running on the Howard stadium track, I heard someone running behind me say, "You're looking good, Coach." I turned as he caught up with me and noticed that it was Adrian Dantley. After conversing for a few moments, Adrian asked me to run some 100-yard wind sprints with him. I told him that I was running a quarter (440 yards) and walking a quarter four or five times. I invited him to join me, but he decided to run the 100-yard wind sprints instead and I continued running my quarters.

A day or so later, Adrian visited me in my office, and we shared some experiences about our individual involvement in sports as well as our experiences together as player and coach. I recalled that he had broken his wrist during his previous NBA season, and I inquired about his wrist. He held his hand up, began flexing his wrist, and said, "It's still a little sore and stiff." I told him that I would give him an Exer-Stik to work out with and if he used it on a regular basis and worked with it as hard as he did with his other exercises, his wrist would be better than new. When I saw him the next day, I gave him the Exer-Stik. He asked what size shoe I wore. I told him and some time later, he reciprocated by giving me a pair of running shoes. He also went back to play basketball in the NBA the following season and picked up where he left off as a player and again was one of the leading scorers in the league. Adrian became the Comeback Player of the Year in 1984.

Photo by Don Baker
After winning a trophy Billy Coward walks off the tennis court with Phil Chenier, former Washington Bullets star and current Washington Wizards TV commentator, 1983

Photo by Don Baker
L-R: Jim "Bad News" Barnes, Bill Martin, Sam Jones, Harold Bell, Billy Coward, Ken Beatrice and Don Washington pose for picture after the 7th Annual Inside Sports Benefit Celebrity Tennis Tournament won by doubles team of Sam Jones and Billy Coward in 1983

B. Coward's Personal Collection
Members of the 1st CIAA Tournament Basketball Champions (1946) receive plaques after being inducted into the CIAA Hall of Fame, L-R:
Coach Leroy Walker, Alex Rivera, Coach John McClendon

B. Coward's Personal Collection
Members of the 1st CIAA Tournament Basketball Champions (1946)
From L-R: Welcome T. Moten, Frank Galbreath, Richard Miller,
Robert Herrin, Aubrey Stanley, Russell Williams, Carl Galbreath

Chapter 11

IN JUNE OF 1993, when I retired from Howard University and from my position as administrator in charge of recreational activities for students, faculty, and staff, a terrific retirement party was given on my behalf. At that party I was roasted by colleagues, friends, and family members, including master of ceremonies Glenn Harris. Other roasters included my brother, Leon; my brother-in-law, Charles "Chuck" Baron; Albert "Needle Head" Smith, a long-time friend; Leo Miles; Richard Mosby; Gary Washington; Frank Bolden; and Donald Lipscomb. Each of them seemed to relish the opportunity to roast me in this venue. I'll have to admit that it was hilarious. Even as the intended target, I enjoyed the humor.

After my retirement, Steve Wilson, the head football coach at Howard, asked me if I would come out and assist him as the coach for the kickers on the team. Based on previous conversations, he knew my response would be "Yes." Steve also knew that I was in college (North Carolina College in Durham) when his father, "Touchdown" Tommy Wilson, was playing football at Hillside High School in Durham. Tommy later went on to play professionally in the NFL as a running back with the Los Angeles Rams, the Cleveland Browns, and the Minnesota Vikings.

Prior to becoming the head football coach at Howard, Steve played for the university. During his senior year of eligibility in 1978, he was named All-MEAC and Honorable Mention All-American. He was signed as a free agent by the Dallas Cowboys in 1979 and played for three years with that team. He moved on and played for seven years with the Denver Broncos. Steve put together a formidable coaching staff, including Rayford "Ray" Petty as defensive coordinator; A.C. Cauthorn as offensive coordinator and quarterback coach; and other coaches, like Sanders Shiver, who worked with the defensive line. Sanders played with the Baltimore Colts and Miami Dolphins. Fred Dean, the offensive line coach, played for the Chicago Bears and the Washington Redskins. He was one of the original linemen called "The Hogs" when Washington won the Super Bowl in 1982. Rickie Harris was Steve's receiver coach. Rickie played for the Washington Redskins when they were coached by Vince Lombardi in 1969. Otis Wonsley was the running-back coach. Otis also played for the Washington Redskins, and his teammate John Riggins gave him credit for blocking many opponents, enabling Riggins to gain a lot of yardage during his tenure. Mack Alston, the end coach, played tight-end with the Redskins. Greg Butler, the defensive-back coach, played defensive back for the Los Angeles Rams and also for the Edmonton Eskimos in the Canadian Football League (CFL). Ron Springs, the offensive-back coach, was a backfield mate of Tony Dorsett when both played for the Dallas Cowboys. The 1993 Howard Bison was co-captained by quarterback Jay "Sky" Walker and wide receiver Gary "Flea" Harrell. Jay had previously enrolled at Long Beach State in California, where he played football and was coached by George Allen, the former Washington Redskin's coach. Unfortunately, George Allen died, and Jay made the decision to transfer to Howard.

On the first day of practice for the 1993 football season, Steve introduced me to the kickers. They were Jason DeCuir and Ruben Ruiz, both freshmen. Jason had played for a catholic high school in Baton Rouge and Ruben for Hallendale High School in Fort Lauderdale, Florida. Jason was a walk-on for the team, and Ruben had been recruited by assistant coach, Ruben Carter. Ruben was from Fort Lauderdale also. He was an All-American at Miami and played nose tackle professionally for the Denver Broncos from 1975 to 1986. Ruben's son, Andre Carter, played professionally for the San Francisco 49ers, the Washington Redskins, and the New England Patriots. Ruben coached at Howard starting in 1989 and left prior to the beginning of the 1993 practice session.

After meeting them, I asked if they were good kickers, and both of them replied, "Yes." I told them I wanted to make certain they had confidence in their abilities. And when I asked, I wanted their response to reflect their confidence in themselves and reassure everyone else. One of the first things that I talked to them about was a potential game situation: It is fourth down, and we are deep in our own territory. The ball is on our 6-yard line. We are in punt formation, and the center snaps the football back to the punter wide left and on the ground, the ball enters the end zone. What should the punter do?

The answer should have been: The punter should kick the ball out of the back of the end zone for a safety. If the opposing team recovers the football in the end zone, it would be a touchdown and six points for the opposing team. If the kicker or one of his teammates recovers the football and is tackled in the end zone by the opposing team, it would be ruled a safety and two points for the opposing team. However, if the kicker kicks the football behind and out of the end zone, it would be ruled a safety and two points would be scored for the opposing team.

After going over some rules and other game-like situations with the kickers, they were told to loosen up by jogging around the football field, stretch, and then join the rest of the fellows in team exercises. This became a part of our practice regimen, which also included a workout with the Exer-Genie and the Lifeline Gym. Then we worked on simulated snaps from center with me throwing the football underhanded and the throws were high, low, wide, and bouncing off the ground. The kickers would catch the football and go through a punting motion. We also worked on fundamental form, technique, and steps for kicking extra points, field goals, kickoffs, and on-side kicks. Both Ruben and Jason worked on all facets of the kicking game, in case one got injured, the other could take his place. However, Ruben was the primary punter and Jason the primary kickoff, extra-point, and field-goal kicker.

We opened our 1993 football season by playing Virginia Union at home in Greene Stadium. Early in the game, Howard had possession of the football deep in Howard territory. On fourth down, we were forced to punt. We were in punt formation, and Ruben was waiting for the snap from the center. When the center snapped the football, it went over Ruben's head into the end zone. Ruben ran after the football and kicked it out of the back of the end zone for a safety and two points. I thought that was the turning point in that game, because had Union recovered the football in the end zone for a touchdown, it could have been a momentum changer for them. Fortunately for Howard, what was a close scoring ballgame at that point turned into a 34-9 victory for us.

The following Monday at practice, A.C. Cauthorn, the quarterback and wide receiver coach, came up to me and said, "Billy, did you tell that freshman (referring to Ruben) to kick the football out of the end zone?" I responded, "No, that was a decision he made." A.C. remarked in amazement, "For a freshman to make a decision like that in a situation like that was very mature." I then told A.C. in the first conversation I had with the kickers, we talked about situations such as those that might come up during the course of a game and what they should do if and when the situation arose. But I also made certain that A.C. knew that the decision to kick the ball out of the end zone was Ruben's.

Our next game was another home game against Winston-Salem State. The Bison were able to come out victoriously again with a 31-10 score. Alcorn State University in Mississippi was our next opponent. The game was played in Busch Memorial Stadium in St. Louis at the Gateway Classic. I recall how we had to get up at 4:00 A.M. on a Friday morning to be on Howard's campus in order to get on the buses that would take us to the airport to catch a flight to St. Louis. After arriving at the airport in St. Louis, we boarded buses to take us to the Marriott Hotel downtown. As we were traveling to the hotel, we saw the devastation of the city that had been caused by a recent hurricane. Buildings had been toppled, graves in a cemetery had been displaced, headstones ripped from their positions, and caskets dislodged from their graves. The next morning, we walked from the Marriott to Busch Stadium. In front of the stadium was a statute of Stan Musial, one of the all-time great players in Major League baseball who played for the St. Louis Cardinals.

At game time, we knew we were playing an opposing team with a gifted quarterback, Alcorn's All-American Steve McNair. We were mentally prepared for a tough football game because the Bison's starting quarterback, Jay Walker, had sustained a badly sprained ankle in the previous game against Winston-Salem. Because of Jay's injury, Pep Hamilton, our sophomore quarterback, got the start. Pep turned in a good job early in the game, but McNair and the rest of the Alcorn team threatened to make the game a rout. At that point, Howard's coach, Steve Wilson, called on Jay Walker. Jay, along with Jimmy Cunningham, who had a great game returning kicks including one for a touchdown, and fullback Rupert Grant, who was the leading ground gainer for Howard and scored a touchdown in the game, were instrumental in leading the Bison to a 38-36 come-from-behind victory over Alcorn. Our next opponent during that season was Florida A&M in Tallahassee. The Rattlers were ranked nationally. Jay, Jimmy, and Rupert had back-to-back good games statistically, and as a result, we won that game 32-13.

For the second week in a row, the Bison faced a Florida team. We traveled to Daytona Beach to play Bethune-Cookman. Incidentally, my grandmother, Jane Elizabeth Dudley Avant, told me that she and Mary McCloud Bethune, one of the founders of Bethune-Cookman College, were roommates when they were students at Barbara Scotia College in Concord, NC. I remember that the game was played on a rainy day with the threat of thunderstorms throughout the game. The Bison defense rose to the occasion on several different times during the game to stymie the Bethune-Cookman offensive advance. Neal Downing, a safety for the Bison, was able to force a fumble and recover the football in the end zone for a touchdown. The final score was Howard 21, Bethune-Cookman 7.

Towson State University was next on Howard's schedule. I was told that Howard had not defeated Towson in four previous meetings. I also knew Adrian Dantley had become the assistant coach for the Towson Tigers basketball team. The Howard football team traveled to Towson by bus, with one bus for the offense and another for the defense. The bus on which the defensive team and I rode pulled up at the gymnasium on Towson's campus and got off. As we entered the gym, I noticed the Towson basketball team was practicing. I asked one of the players if Coach Dantley was around, and was told that he was. When I saw Adrian, he said to me, "I was just thinking about you. I've got the basketball players running a five and six quarters, and man, that's hard." I smiled and said, "I know it."

After the game started, the Tigers jumped out to a 21-0 lead. Towson's big running back was having an outstanding game as he frequently picked up large chunks of yards early in the game. Not to be outdone, Jay Walker appeared poised and confident and led the Bison back time and time again. With the score 41-31 in Towson's favor and less than six minutes left in the game, Jay and his teammates went to work. Howard scored another touchdown and kicked the extra point to make the score 41-38. After the ensuing kickoff, the Bison defense held and got the ball back on their own 35-yard line with 59 seconds remaining on the clock. Jay engineered a drive to the 9-yard line with 8 seconds remaining in the game. With time for only one more play, Jay faded back to pass and pumped once to the right side of the field, then pumped once to the left side of the field, and came back to the right side of the field and passed the football to a waiting Germaine Kohn for a touchdown with no time left on the clock. The final score was Howard 44, Towson 41. Our entire team was so jubilant after the victory – they congratulated each other, slapping backs, and giving hi-fives. I was overcome with emotion to the point that I shed a few tears of joy at the thought that we had pulled off a very tough game. Ron Springs saw me and said, "Look at Billy, just crying like a baby." Incidentally, Ron's son, Shaun, played football locally at Springbrook High School in Silver Spring, in college at Ohio State, and professionally with the Seattle Seahawks, the Washington Redskins, and the New England Patriots.

North Carolina A&T was next on our schedule. Unfortunately, the Aggies had beaten the Bison the last four times they had played. It was their homecoming, and 26,000 fans packed their stadium. The game was also televised on BET. Jesse Jackson was a graduate of A&T and had played quarterback on the Aggies football team. On the day of our game, he was parading around the field carrying the A&T flag. Howard started out with an early lead in this game with a score of 21-7. But the Aggies fought back early in the fourth quarter to gain a 35-21 lead. Behind by two touchdowns and two extra points, Jay Walker began showing his masterful leadership and tied the score 35-35 at the end of regulation play. Going into overtime, the Aggies won the flip of the coin to see who would take possession first. A&T had four downs from the 25-yard line to score, but the Bison defense rose to the occasion and prevented them from scoring. Howard then had its opportunity. The football was placed on the 25-yard line, first down and goal to go. Throughout the game, A&T's defense had been playing to stop the Howard passing attack. But on the first play in overtime, the Bison came out in a passing formation, and the A&T defense was again set up to stop the pass. This defense left a large gap in the center, and Jay recognized this right away. As he set up to take the snap from the center in a spread passing formation, he took the snap from the center and followed him through the gap for a 25-yard touchdown. Final score: Howard 41, A&T 35. The victory was a very impressive come-from-behind win, and Jay Walker again led the Bison to what looked like an impossible task.

Morehouse was our next opponent, and to our credit, Howard came out victorious again with a 34-9 win. South Carolina State, who had frequently been a formidable foe in the past, was the next opponent. But this time, Howard was able to rise to the task and came out with a 30-14 victory. Next on our schedule was Morgan State in Hughes Stadium on Morgan's campus. With an awesome display of offensive power, the Bears' defense was dismantled as the Bison rolled to a 66-37 win in that game. The next stop was a game played in Dover, Delaware, against Delaware State. Instead of the Hornets stinging the Bison that year, the Bison continued to roll with a 20-point victory: 53-33.

That football season was quite significant for Howard because it was the first time the football team had gone undefeated during the regular MEAC season with a very impressive 11-0 record. By doing so, Howard captured its first ever Mid-Eastern Athletic Conference title. By winning the MEAC title, this qualified the Bison to play in the NCAA I-AA playoffs, where they played Marshall University in Huntington, West Virginia. Marshall was the NCAA

I-AA defending champion who ended up defeating us in that game 28-14. However, Howard was crowned the National Black College Football Champions. Additionally, there were several honors and accolades received by Jay Walker as he was named the MEAC Player of the Year, the Touchdown Club Quarter Back of the Year, and *Sports Illustrated* I-AA Player of the Year. Jay's roommate, Gary "Flea" Harrell, was named to the First Team All-MEAC as a wide receiver and kick-return specialist. Gary was also selected as the Pigskin Club's Metro Player of the Year. Steve Wilson was selected as the MEAC Coach of the Year, the Sheridan Black Network Coach of the Year, and the Pigskin Club's Coach of the Year.

Jay took his talent to the NFL, where he played football for two years with the New England Patriots and then two years with the Minnesota Vikings. While in school at Howard, he majored in political science. In 2007 he ran for delegate of the 26th legislative district of Maryland and won a seat in the Maryland House of Delegates. He also became a sports commentator on ESPNU, where he is currently a color analyst for the football games.

After graduating from Howard, Gary played professional football with the New York Giants for four years and then served as an assistant coach at Texas Southern, Florida A&M, and Bowie State and returned to his alma mater as the head football coach in 2011.

In 1994 the Greater Washington Urban League started promoting the First Annual Greater Washington Urban League Football Classic. The Howard University Bison opposed the Hampton University Pirates in that game. The game was played at Robert F. Kennedy Stadium. This was a resurrection of the football era of the Capital Classic in the 1940s and 1950s. On the day before the football game, a luncheon was held at the Grand Hyatt Hotel. Representatives from both universities' administration and athletic departments were in attendance. Jim Vance, a news anchor from NBC Channel 4 in Washington was the MC. Jim introduced me as one of the speakers and told the audience that my father, John E. "Jerry" Coward, was one of the originators of the Capital Classic. I was then asked to give an overview of the Capital Classic during the 1940s and 1950s. The proceeds from the Classic went to the universities' athletic and educational funds and also to support the various programs of the Urban League.

During the 1994 and 1995 football seasons, the Bison football team fell to mediocrity and had to reload to get back to the winning ways of the 1993 football season. The 1994 record was 4 wins and 7 losses. The 1995 record improved to one game over .500 with 6 wins and 5 losses. But even then, I saw a lot of growth and development in the kickers, Rubin Ruiz and Jason DeCuir, the players with whom I had primary responsibility as the kicking coach. They continued to work hard in their daily training daily as they had in previous years by loosening up as they jogged a couple of laps around the football field then worked through a variety of stretching movements before going through the kicking and punting motions. Workouts with the Exer-Genie and the Lifeline apparatus were used to strengthen and stretch the leg muscles in particular. After that, we would sprint the length of the football field and walk across the end zone. Then they sprinted the length of the football field again until we had sprinted the length of the field six times. I always sprinted along with them. Afterward, we then proceeded to work on fundamental techniques of punting, kickoffs, extra points, and field-goal kicking. Twice a week we went to the weight room to lift weights; as they worked out so did I. I felt that Ruben was talented enough to be a running back on offense or a linebacker on defense. He had tremendous leg drive and a very explosive start, making him ideal, in my mind, to be a running back on offense. Defensively, he was a very physical player and seemed to thrive on making contact and tackling ball carriers. This point was made evident during the course of several football games when he punted to the opposing team and the other team's player returning the punt got away from all the players on our team. Ruben was the last player between the punt returner and a touchdown. Ruben not only stopped the punt returner but met him with such force that he picked him up and drove him in the opposite direction in making the tackle. On a couple of occasions, former players so impressed with his tackling came up to me and inquired about him. They asked, "Where did you get that kicker from, Coach?" I could only smile. Ruben could have been an outstanding linebacker also because he was a punishing tackler.

I remember one day during practice when Ruben began practicing with the running backs and they were engaged in some physical drills. Coach Wilson came up to him and said in a very firm voice, "Get out of there. What are you trying to do?" Steve didn't want to risk injury to either one of his kickers. Ruben came over to the sideline where I was standing and, for several minutes, looked very solemn and depressed. So, I asked him what was wrong, and he replied, "Coach got into my head." He wanted to play in other aspects of the game so much either offensively or defensively, not only as a kicker. But it was not to be.

Jason had an analytical mind. I remember one day at practice when he was having difficulty making field goals. He would show the player who would hold the football the spot he wanted the football placed, then take his usual three steps straight back and two steps to the side. As soon as the center snapped the ball back to the holder, Jason took his two steps forward and kicked the football soccer-style toward the goal post. Frequently he was pulling the football wide of the goal post. I didn't notice any deviation in his kicking motion as I watched him several times, but the football continued to be kicked wide of the goal post. This went on for a day or two. After kicking practice, we went to the sideline, and I saw Jason staring at the ground seemingly in deep thought, trying to figure out why he was constantly kicking the football wide of the goal posts. At the next practice, he went through his regular routine in kicking field goals. As he continued to practice, he became more consistent again in making most of his field-goal attempts. He told me that as the center snapped the football to the holder, he was moving his feet slightly and then taking his regular two steps forward in his approach to kick the football. That movement was so subtle that I didn't notice it. In eliminating the slight movement of his feet prior to the two-step approach to the football, Jason became constant again with his field-goal kicking. He was able to analyze and correct his own mistake.

The emergence of Ted White to the football program at Howard brought about a new perspective for the Bison. Ted came to Howard with his high school teammate and running back Tyrone Lewis from Baton Rouge in 1994. Ted was a quarterback and stood 6'4" tall. He possessed tremendous arm strength which was evident whenever he passed the football. Ted was redshirted his first year on campus. During the practices of the 1994 football season and spring practice of 1995, I saw an incredible improvement in his knowledge of the system; his fundamentals and technique at the quarterback position; and his leadership through example demonstrated in practice and game situations. I don't recall in my experience as a coach any one athlete making so much progress in such a short period of time.

We opened the 1996 football season playing against Marshall in Huntington. The Thundering Herd, as they are called, were the 1995 NCAA Division I-AA national champions. That day they seemed to be operating on all cylinders offensively and, unfortunately for us, beat us 55-27. Our next game, however, was against the Hampton Pirates in the Greater Washington Urban League Football Classic at RFK Stadium, a game in which we fared better than in the previous one against Marshall. The Bison came out on top by beating the Pirates 26-7. The year before Howard had met Hampton in the same football classic and won the game 34-22. This was becoming something of a rivalry between the two teams and often prompted the question: Which was the real HU, Howard University or Hampton University?

The Virginia State Trojans were our next opponents. The game was played on Howard's campus at Greene Stadium. Once again Howard came out on top – 31-7. We were hoping to extend our winning streak when we traveled to Tallahassee to play Florida A&M. This game really stands out in my mind because with very little time left to play in the game, the Rattlers led 21-20. Coach Wilson sent in the field-goal unit, hoping to seize the lead at this point. Jason DeCuir, the kicker, who had been "Mister Clutch" in the past by kicking field goals late in the game to give Howard the win, ended up missing the field goal, and Florida won the game by one point. After the game, Jason took the loss and the missed field-goal attempt very hard. In fact he was despondent for a long time after the game but more than made up for it in future games.

At this point, we were only four games into our 1996 football schedule and so far were 2-2 but looking ahead with optimism. Bethune-Cookman came to Washington, and the Bison offense began to flex its muscles; it overpowered the Wildcats by a score of 61-21. Our next encounter was against Morehouse in Atlanta. The Bison were again operating on all cylinders offensively and defensively. We routed Morehouse 49-0 and moved on to play North Carolina A&T in Howard's homecoming game. Again the defense proved to be up to the task of keeping the opposition out of the end zone and allowed the Aggies only one field goal. Howard triumphed again 38-3. At this point, the team was pumped up and really ready to play. Our next opponent was Norfolk State in a game on Howard's campus. There was no letup in that game; Norfolk received a 42-14 thumping from the mighty Bison. It seemed that we were on a roll, and the players appeared to be more and more confident with each win.

Our next opponents were the South Carolina State Bulldogs on their home turf in Orangeburg, South Carolina. The Bison defense was once again turned up a notch as they held the Bulldogs to a field goal, giving Howard a 23-3 win. Our schedule for the season was winding down at this point when we faced the Morgan State Bears on Howard's playground in Greene Stadium. Once again Howard gave the opposing team a real thrashing by winning 49-0. Our final game was also played on Howard's campus against Delaware State, and again the Bison rose to the occasion and spanked the Hornets. The score: Howard 40, Delaware State 21.

With the regular season schedule completed, the Bison football team was invited to play Southern University of Baton Rouge in the McDonald's

Heritage Bowl in the Georgia Dome on December 31 of that year. Southern had won the distinction of being the National Black College Football Champions for 1995 and were the defending National Black College Football Champions.

Howard had three players on the team from Baton Rouge, and they wanted so badly to defeat the Jaguars from their hometown so they would have bragging rights to who had the better team when they returned home. Those players were Ted White, quarterback; Tyrone Lewis, running back; and Jason DeCuir, kicker. Several things that took place during the course of the game stand out in my mind that I will not soon forget. One was the "leadership by example" that I saw in Ted White, not only during the regular football season but in clutch time during this game. Ted led the team from a 24-10 halftime deficit to a 24-24 tie. Included in this surge was an 81-yard touchdown pass to MacArthur Johnson. There was a giant television screen mounted up in the stands behind the end zone in the Georgia Dome. After MacArthur caught the pass from Ted, he seemed to be looking up at the TV screen, watching himself run after he caught the pass, with the defenders from Southern in hot pursuit.

In that game he scored the touchdown; however, in a previous game in which Ted had thrown MacArthur a pass and he was headed for a touchdown, an opposing player caught him from behind, tackled him, and prevented him from making a touchdown. As I watched the play in progress in the previous game, I noticed MacArthur was making the effort to separate from the opposing player by quickly moving his feet forward. But the player caught him and stopped him anyway. When Mac returned to the sideline, I spoke with him and said, "I thought you were moving your feet quickly enough to get some distance between yourself and the defenders, but it appeared that you needed to exaggerate your knee lifts as high as possible and extend your lower leg outward with each stride to make your steps longer to get more separation from your opponent. Try doing that in the future." In the game in the Georgia Dome, I asked MacArthur if he were watching himself running on the giant TV screen, and he responded that he was. "If you were," I continued, "could you see the Southern defenders in hot pursuit?" And he said, "Yes." I then asked if he were exaggerating his knee lift and extending his lower legs with each stride as I had suggested before. His response was, "Uh-huh." In doing so, he made the touchdown that seemed to lift the spirit of the team and inspired them to persevere even more.

At this point in the game, there were approximately seven minutes to play, the score was tied at 24-all, and Howard had possession of the football. All of a sudden I noticed Jason DeCuir, our kicker, loosening up by running back and forth behind our bench and along the sideline. As he was running back and forth, I could hear him say, "He can't out-kick me. I'm going to win this ball-game. Just watch!" Jason had told me that when he went home to Baton Rouge during the summer months, he practiced kicking extra points and field goals. The kicker from Southern practiced along with him during that time. Jason continued to warm up, running along the sideline and repeated over and over, "He can't out-kick me. I'm going to win this ball game." Ted White again did a masterful job of leading the Bison down the field, and with approximately three minutes left to play in the game, Steve Wilson sent Jason in to attempt an 18-yard field goal with Cedric Redding holding. Jason was true to his word – the kick was good, giving Howard a 27-24 lead. The defense held after we kicked off to Southern in the last two minutes or so, and our 3-point lead held, giving us the victory. After the game, I was so emotionally charged that a few tears started rolling from my eyes. Steve's father, "Touchdown" Tommy Wilson, was nearby. I said to him, "Tommy, have you ever seen a sixty-five-year old man cry?" He looked at me and started to smile. However, in the next few moments, he also had tears of joy running down his cheeks.

The next morning, upon our return to Washington, I got a copy of *The Washington Post* newspaper dated January 1, 1997. I turned to the sports section, and on the front page was a picture of Cedric Redden and Jason – Cedric, with his arms raised signaling the kick was good and Jason after he had kicked the winning field goal.

As a result of our seasonal record and winning the Heritage Bowl against Southern, Howard won the Black College National Championship for the second time in four years – first in 1993 and again in 1996. Ted White was selected as the Most Valuable Player in the Heritage Bowl along with a number of other honors he received that year. He was voted to the All-MEAC First Team as well as the Offensive Player of the Year and the I-AA All-American Team. He had set a new record of touchdown passes thrown in a season for Howard with 36; the old record was 24, set by Jay Walker.

The kickers did well in their four-year careers at Howard stretching over a period from 1993 to 1996. Ruben Ruiz made the All-MEAC First Team as a punter in 1994 and again in 1995. Jason DeCuir holds the career-points-after-touchdown record of 130 and 35 field goals. He also was a First Team

All-MEAC selection as a place kicker in 1995, and in 1996 he was also a Sport's View All-American.

During the 1997 football season, the team had a record of 7 wins and 4 losses. Ted was the team leader in the quarterback position. One game is quite memorable, more so than others. That game was against Morehouse in Greene Stadium. Morehouse was coached by Doug Williams, who was in his first year of coaching at Morehouse after spending two years as an assistant football coach at the Naval Academy. Prior to that he was a quarterback for the Washington Redskins and led them to the Super Bowl XXII Championship in 1988. During the Morehouse game, Howard displayed an awesome power both offensively and defensively. The offensive unit scored 52 points, and the defensive unit shutdown Morehouse's offense, rendering them scoreless. Final score: Howard 52, Morehouse 0.

After the game, the broadcaster Charlie Neal, who had provided the play-by-play description of the game, and I were engaged in a conversation with Doug outside the visiting team's locker room in Burr Gymnasium, as he waited for his players to finish dressing. Doug said, "You know, I was responsible for Ted White and Tyrone Lewis coming to Howard." I acknowledged that I was aware of that, having been told by Steve Wilson previously. I'm quite certain Doug must have had mixed emotions about the outcome of the game, knowing he had sent to Howard the quarterback who had just beaten the Morehouse team he was coaching. As we continued to talk, I said to Doug, "I know who is going to Grambling, your alma mater, to take your former football coach Eddie Robinson's place." Eddie was retiring after many successful years as Grambling's coach. Doug asked who I thought it might be. I pointed to him and said, "You!" Doug asked how I had figured that out. I said, "Bob Piper is a friend of yours, right?" Doug acknowledged that he was. I said, "Bob Piper was your agent while you were playing football with the Redskins, wasn't he?" Doug said, "Yes." "And Bob Piper is now the athletic director at Grambling, isn't he?" Doug nodded in agreement. Given those circumstances, it seemed obvious to me that Doug would certainly be on a very short list for consideration for the job. So I repeated what I had said to him before, "I know who will be the next football coach at Grambling – you!" He looked at me and smiled. He did succeed Eddie Robinson and became the football coach at Grambling prior to the beginning of the 1998 football season.

During the 1998 football season, the Bison were again led by quarterback Ted "Sweet Flight" White. Howard finished with a record identical to the record of the previous year –7 wins and 4 losses. The most significant feat that year in my thinking, was in a home game against Norfolk State in which Ted had what might have been his most significant game as a Bison: he completed 22 of 32 passes and 8 touchdowns. The eight touchdowns were a new Howard record and also a new MEAC record.

During the 1999 football season, the Bison win-loss record slipped to 5 wins and 6 losses, although the offense was able to score 21 points or more a game with the exception of the game against North Carolina A&T. The Aggies defense held Howard scoreless while they scored 51 points. The Bison defense was porous and allowed the opponents to score 23 points or more, resulting in more losses than wins for Howard that year.

Several young men who played football at Howard while I was a member of the coaching staff later played in the NFL. Some of them were Jay "Sky" Walker, New England Patriots and Minnesota Vikings; Gary "Flea" Harrell, New York Giants; Billy Jenkins, Saint Louis Rams, Denver Broncos, and Buffalo Bills; Ted "Sweet Flight" White, Kansas City Chiefs, Tampa Bay Buccaneers, and Jacksonville Jaguars; Marques Douglas, Baltimore Ravens and New Orleans Saints; Tracy White, Seattle Seahawks and New England Patriots; Elijah Thurmon, Philadelphia Eagles and Oakland Raiders; Pep Hamilton, who became the quarterback coach for the Chicago Bears; Jose White, Minnesota Vikings and Jacksonville Jaguars; and Leonard Stephens, San Diego Chargers and Washington Redskins.

The last football game of the 1999 season, as in previous years, had been scheduled against Delaware State in Dover. This game in particular is etched in my mind because I was asked by the athletic director if I would take over the coaching responsibilities of the basketball team at Howard. Prior to the start of the football game, Hank Ford, the athletic director and a former basketball coach at Hampton when I was the basketball coach at Federal City College in the mid-1970s, told me that Howard's president was looking for someone to take over the reins of the basketball team. I was told that the basketball coach was being replaced for a violation of NCAA and University regulations. Hank asked if I would be interested in taking over on an interim basis. I told him I would have to think about it because 1976 was the last time I had coached basketball. I found out later that A.B. Williamson, the then compliance officer for the athletic department and a former head basketball coach at Howard, had suggested to the president and Hank that I might be interested in becoming the interim basketball coach. I had coached against A.B. when both of us were coaching on the high school level.

After a few days of mulling it over and knowing it would be short term, I offered to help out if and when a final decision were made regarding staff changes in that department. No decision was made immediately, but I was contacted periodically by Hank to reassure me there was still an interest in having me on board. Finally on Friday, January 7, 2000, I received a call from Hank and was told that the president was going to make a decision that day and wanted to know if I could come to the campus as soon as possible. I told him I had reserved court time at the tennis bubble at 16th and Kennedy and was on my way out the door when he called. I asked if he would leave a message in my voice mailbox when a decision had been made, and I would return his call when I returned home. I played for about two hours, and there were three messages from Hank when I returned. Each message was the same: The president had made his decision, and he asked me to come to the gym right away. I returned Hank's call to let him know I was on my way.

When I arrived at the gym, I found out that Hank had already summoned several members of the basketball team to meet with me in one of the classrooms. After being introduced to the players, they had several questions and concerns directed to me. One of the first questions asked was whether I was going to put in new offensive and defensive plays. My response was that my intent was to adjust to the system already in place. I could understand and appreciate their apprehension given the suddenness of the changes in personnel in the program. We left the meeting on a high note, as I had encouraged everyone to think positively.

The very next day, Saturday, January 8, 2000, the basketball team was scheduled to play North Carolina A&T in a home game. The game was televised nationally on the BET network, and the announcers were Charlie Neal and Bobby Dandridge. Charlie did the commentary and Bobby the color. Prior to the game, we discussed our final game plan in the locker room. All of the basketball players seemed to be focused and very upbeat at that moment; however, the team had not won a game in over a year at that point. The realization that the game was being televised nationally and the fact that they had not won a basketball game in more than a year may have been the motivating factor to help them perform to their best potential. When we went out onto the court for our final pre-game warm-up, I sensed a feeling of determination that seemed to resonate with all of the players. That feeling seemed to be transferred into the game. I could see the hustle, determination, and a never-say-die attitude demonstrated by all of the players both defensively and offensively. The fellows persevered throughout the ball game, resulting in a 69-62 win over our opponents. However, there was very little time for us to savor the victory against the Aggies, because the Bulldogs from South Carolina State were our next opponents two days later.

Preparation for the game was done without the benefit of any assistant coaches – none had been hired yet. The Bison were able to put up a very competitive effort during the first half of that game with the Bulldogs, taking a 2-point lead at halftime. During the second half, however, they took advantage of poor shot selection on our part which ended up in missed shots. They made quick outlet passes, leading to several easy fast-break baskets. They took the lead by 8 points and went on to win the game. The final score was South Carolina State 71, Howard 63. After that game, I had a chance to make an assessment of the team, and I found out that two of their former teammates on the team at some point prior to my coming onboard were academically ineligible. Four of the present players were walk-ons. When we practiced and scrimmaged, we invariably had to scrimmage half-court and I had to fill in as one of the players because there was a conflict between when practice was held and the players' class schedules. There may have been six, seven, or eight players absent from practice at any given time. After being without an assistant coach for two weeks, Russell Davis was hired to assist in coaching the team. Throughout the remainder of the season, both of us had to fill in as players when we scrimmaged. Because of several intervening circumstances and a little bad luck, we did not win any more games that season, but we can say that there were no defaults – we did finish playing the balance of the scheduled games.

On Thanksgiving Day, Thursday, November 23, 2000, the District of Columbia Interscholastic Athletic Association (DCIAA) held its 31st Annual Turkey Bowl football game. The game was played at Eastern High School stadium between the Ballou High School Knights and the Dunbar High School Crimson Tide. Both teams had won the right to participate in the game as the result of their winning record during their regular season. The victor would claim the DCIAA championship. At halftime of the game, Johnny Grier, Robert "Bob" Headen, and I were honored for our years of support and interest in the DCIAA programs. Each of us was presented with a plaque as we were recognized on the field during the halftime ceremony. Johnny Grier was a former football and basketball referee in the DCIAA as well as the MEAC and NFL. In fact he was the first African-American referee in the NFL. Bob Headen was an outstanding football coach at Cardozo and H.D. Woodson as well as the girls' basketball coach at Woodson. Dunbar won the game; the final score was 35-12.

On June 16, 2001, of the following year, I was privileged to be inducted into the DC Coaches Hall of Fame. This induction was held at the La Fontaine Bleu, a well-known local venue in New Carrolton, Maryland. I, along with several other inductees, was awarded a plaque in recognition of my contribution as a longtime successful coach in the DCPS. I was humbled, and as I previously indicated, privileged to be offered an opportunity to become a part of the DCPS Coaches Hall of Fame.

In the fall of 2000, I did not return to coaching football; instead I retired for the third time and began to enjoy a life of leisure activities. I continued to play tennis and work out regularly. For the most part, these activities took place at the Aspen Hill Club (AHC) in Silver Spring. I again played on a tennis team in the Montgomery County Super Senior League representing the club against other teams in the area. My wife, Tamara, was also active playing tennis two or three time a week at the club. When she was scheduled to play tennis at the club, I was usually working out in the AHC fitness center there. In 2006 I stopped playing tennis altogether because I tore my rotator cuff on my left shoulder. Because I am left-handed, this inhibited me from continuing to play a sport that I had enjoyed for years. Nonetheless, I didn't let this stop me from exercising. I continued to tell myself, "Don't let what you cannot do interfere with what you can do" – a philosophy I continue to live by each day.

Occasionally while exercising in the fitness center, I saw Dinitri Dantley, Adrian Dantley's wife. She frequented the fitness center on a regular basis. She often mentioned Adrian and kept me abreast of how he was doing. At that time he was the assistant basketball coach for the Denver Nuggets of the NBA. During the winter of 2007, I was exercising at the club one day and saw Dinitri. She had a big smile on her face, as usual. As long as I have known her, she has always displayed a very pleasant demeanor, but she seemed to be more upbeat than usual this particular day. She told me that the Utah Jazz were finally going to retire Adrian's jersey and he wanted to know if I would be interested in going out to Salt Lake City to attend his jersey retirement ceremony. How could I have turned down such an invitation? To me, it was an honor to have been invited to attend this special event celebrating Adrian's contributions to the Utah Jazz as an NBA player. I thought it was quite nice of Adrian to invite me to attend his jersey retirement ceremony along with members of his family, some of his close friends, Morgan Wootten, his high school coach at DeMatha, and Mrs. Wootten – Kathy. The Utah Jazz organization took care of all of the expenses for the group, including the airplane flight to Salt Lake City from Baltimore-Washington International Airport and transportation to and from the airport to the hotel. We stayed at a hotel across the street from the Energy Solutions Arena.

The affair was held on April 11, 2007, the same day the Utah Jazz was scheduled to play the Denver Nuggets. Adrian was an assistant coach for the Nuggets. The reception was held prior to the actual jersey retirement ceremony in the Energy Solutions Arena. "Hot Rod" Huntley was the MC for the event. Several members of the Utah Jazz organization were scheduled speakers to offer tributes to Adrian. His former teammate Ron Boone said, "He is the best 'Little Big Man' I have ever seen play with his back to the basket." Adrian's former coaches Tom Nissalke and Frank Layden said that he had great footwork, and Nissalke also added that A.D. had great fundamentals.

Adrian had played for the Jazz for seven seasons from 1979 to 1986, and he had received several awards during that time: He was named to the All-NBA Second Team in 1981 and again in 1984; shared the NBA record for most free-throws (28) made in a game; he was a six-time NBA All-Star from 1980 to 1986; led the NBA in scoring twice in 1980-81 and 1983-84; and voted the Comeback Player of the Year in 1984. With all the honors he had received when he was a member of the Jazz basketball team, there was much speculation by the fans and some local sportswriters about if and when the Jazz organization would honor him for his outstanding contributions to the team. It had been twenty-one years before the Jazz finally retired his jersey, as 1986 was Adrian's last year with the Jazz.

When Morgan Wootten spoke, he indicated how dedicated Adrian had been and what a hard worker he was. Morgan mentioned that during one Christmas holiday when Adrian was a student at DeMatha, he came to his house and asked for the keys to the gym because he wanted to practice. Morgan also said Adrian was the best basketball player he had ever coached. When Frank Layden spoke, he mentioned that he was partly responsible for Adrian's jersey not being retired earlier. However, when Larry Miller, the owner of the team, spoke on Adrian's behalf, he became emotional and cried, then said he was responsible for the delay in the retirement of the jersey. He praised Adrian for his contribution to the Utah Jazz team.

Later that day after the reception, the Jazz played the Denver Nuggets in the same building. There was a capacity crowd on hand for the game and for Adrian's jersey retirement ceremony, held during halftime. Each fan in attendance was given a free t-shirt with the inscription "Fans 4 Dantley" on the front. His jersey number while playing for Utah was number 4. While passing through the crowd on my way to my seat, the crowd seemed upbeat, and I overheard a couple of the fans commenting that this event was a long time coming and his jersey should have been retired a long time ago.

All of the participants in the jersey-retirement ceremony were advised to report downstairs at the end of the first quarter of the game to assemble under the stands in a designated room. In addition to Adrian's family, the participants included his friends and former coaches. Once the first half of the game ended and the teams had left the court, the participants were asked to proceed to the court. As we did, the public-address announcer welcomed the fans to the halftime and jersey-retirement ceremony. As we walked onto the floor, he introduced us individually and the fans began to applaud. Once we were seated, Morgan spoke first and said pretty much the same thing he had mentioned at the reception – Adrian was the best basketball player he had ever coached. The crowd responded with a tremendous ovation. The announcer introduced Adrian's mother Virginia, his aunt Rosie and his wife Dinitri. After Morgan spoke, Sam Battizone, the original owner of the Jazz when they moved from New Orleans to Salt Lake City, spoke as well as Layden, John Stockton (who spoke on behalf of Adrian's teammates) and Larry Miller. All of them praised Adrian for his outstanding contribution to the Utah Jazz.

Adrian was introduced and received a tremendous standing ovation. His first comment was that he was wondering if this day would ever come. He mentioned that a couple of the fellows who played with the Nuggets, Carmelo Anthony and Marcus Camby, used to say to him, "You couldn't have been but so good because your jersey isn't hanging up in the rafters." Adrian said that he wouldn't have to hear that anymore after that night. He went on to thank everyone who helped make his jersey retirement event possible. It was a special event and a much deserved one for Adrian.

After Adrian's jersey retirement, there was some concern by some friends and family members if he would ever be enshrined in the Basketball Hall of Fame in Springfield, MA. I recall one day several months after his jersey retirement when I ran into Dinitri again in the fitness center at the Aspen Hill Racquet Club. We talked, and she filled me in about how things were going with Adrian as an assistant coach with the Denver Nuggets. She asked me then if I thought he would ever be inducted into the Hall of Fame. My response was, "Can they stop tomorrow from coming?" She smiled but had a right to be concerned because Adrian had been a finalist to enter the Hall of Fame on six different occasions. On each occasion, he was eager to enter and so disappointed when it didn't become a reality. However, he did eventually receive a call from the Hall of Fame acknowledging that he would be enshrined in the Class of 2008. His time had come. On Friday, September 5, 2008, in Springfield, the Basketball Hall of Fame Class of 2008 was enshrined. Adrian's family and several of his friends and I attended the ceremony. Other individuals inducted included William Davidson, Patrick Ewing, Hakeem Olajuwon, Pat Riley, Cathy Rush, and Dick Vitale.

Davidson was recognized for his contribution to basketball as the owner of the Detroit Pistons. He was the first owner of an NBA team to buy an airplane to transport his team around to play other NBA teams. Ewing was honored for his outstanding play for the New York Knicks. Olajuwon was recognized and honored for his superior basketball skills as a member of the Houston Rockets. In 1994 he was the Most Valuable Player of the Year, Defensive Player of the Year during the regular season, and MVP of the finals. He is the only player in NBA history to achieve that combination of awards. Riley was acknowledged for his outstanding contributions to the NBA and coaching the Los Angeles Lakers, the New York Knicks, and the Miami Heat. Rush was recognized for her achievement in coaching Immaculata Pennsylvania College women's team to 149 wins and only 15 losses and for having won three Association of Intercollegiate Athletics for Women (AIAW) national titles in seven years. Vitale was honored for his sports reporting and promoting college basketball on ESPN. Adrian was recognized for being a gold medalist in the 1976 Olympics; Rookie-of-the-Year in the NBA in 1977; leading the NBA in scoring twice, once in 1980-81 and again in 1983-84; Comeback Player of the NBA in 1984; six-time NBA All-Star 1980-1982 and 1984-1986; named to the NBA's 50th Anniversary All Time Team; and shares the NBA record for most free throws.

Although the enshrinement of the Class of 2008 into the Hall of Fame took place on Friday, September 5, several members of Adrian's family, friends, and I traveled to Springfield the day before on Thursday, September 4. This was my first time visiting the Hall of Fame and my first exposure to so many celebrity basketball players and other individuals affiliated with professional basketball. I got a chance to interact with many of them. Most of them I had not met before but recognized their names from my many years of involvement in basketball. During my conversations with several of them, I found out that we knew some of the same people. I had an opportunity to talk with John Chaney, the former coach at Temple, and Meadowlark Lemon, the crown prince of basketball with the Harlem Globetrotters. While we were conversing, Rick Barry, a former NBA player, joined us and told us that he had just returned from his vacation, a fishing trip to Alaska. I mentioned to him that I had the pleasure of going on a cruise that past summer to Alaska also. I told Meadowlark that I had attended North Carolina College with his high school coach, Harold Hunter. Meadowlark thought for a moment, then told me that he remembered Harold and recalled him having the members of the team playing three men on a team full-court. The first team to score ten points would win and the loser would stay on the court to play the next team. That would help get the players motivated and, hopefully, develop a winning attitude. I told him I had the fellows whom I coached over the years, playing the same game.

I also saw and talked with Marques Haynes, the world-famous dribbler with the Harlem Globetrotters. I first met Marques back in the 1950s after a game he played in at the Uline Arena. He was visiting an uncle who owned a store on 9th Street in the District. He is also a fraternity brother of mine (Kappa Alpha Psi). Fred "Curley" Neal, the fellow who succeeded Marques as the outstanding dribbler with the Globetrotters, was also in attendance. Curley attended Johnson C. Smith University and he told me he was coached by Eddie McGirt, a cousin of my sister-in-law. David Thompson was there as well. I told him I was in Greensboro when he carried his team, North Carolina State, to the NCAA Championship in 1974. I told David that James "Beannie" Howell, who is a close friend of mine, and who had refereed that game, was the first African-American referee to officiate an NCAA championship game. Another attendee, Earl Lloyd, whom I have mentioned previously, and I exchanged some pleasantries about mutual friends. I met James Worthy who played with the Lakers. I mentioned that I knew his brother, Dan, who was an administrator in the athletic department at my alma mater, North Carolina Central University. I also mentioned that his high school principal in Gastonia, NC, Robert "R.O." Mason, and I played football together at NCCU.

During one of the scheduled events on Thursday, September 4, 2008, David Dupree, who used to write about high school sports for *The Washington Post* and wrote a few articles on games that I coached at Bell Vocational High School and Federal City College, was an award recipient. David received the Curt Gowdy Print Media award for his contribution to basketball through his newspaper articles. Dupree was also once a panelist on the "George Michael Sports Machine Show" on NBC Channel 4 in Washington for years. Sonny Hill of Philadelphia was also honored. He received the Mannie Jackson Spirit Award for his personal contributions to the game of basketball. Other basketball celebrities whom I recognized at the ceremony were Dave Bing, John Thompson, Dominique Wilkins, Earl Monroe, Moses Malone, Earvin "Magic" Johnson, Bailey Howell, Joe Dumars, Coach Chuck Daly and Coach Mike Brea of Notre Dame.

On Friday, November 7, 2008, I was invited to attend a reception for Major League Baseball heroes of World War II. The event was held at the new Washington Nationals Stadium in the Presidents Club which is located under the stands and behind home plate. Among those who were being honored were Hall of Famer Bob Feller of the Cleveland Indians; Monte Irvin of the New York Giants; and Ralph Kiner of the Pittsburgh Pirates. Other baseball celebrities who were there included Lou Brissie, Jerry Coleman and Joe Anders. Johnny Holliday, who was the MC at this event, announced that on that day Bob Feller was celebrating his 90th birthday. At the end of the ceremony, I got an opportunity to chat with Irving and Feller and had photos taken with each of them. While chatting with Irving I showed him a picture of myself as the batboy for the Homestead Grays which included Luke Easter, who was shown in the photo just after hitting a home run. Right away, he recognized both Luke and Wilmer and while pointing to each of them called their names. I mentioned that I was also his batboy when the Negro National League All-Stars played the Negro American League All-Stars here in Washington at the old Griffith Stadium in 1946. We reminisced and mentioned a lot of names of the outstanding players who played in that game and several of the players eventually played in the Major League, as he did. I also told Monte that I knew his brother, Cal Irvin and remembered seeing him play football and basketball when he was a member of the Morgan State College Bears. I mentioned to him that I knew Clarence "Big House" Gaines who was a teammate of Cal's in both football and basketball also. Cal Irvin later became the basketball coach at Johnson C. Smith in Charlotte and at North Carolina A&T in Greensboro. Big House became the basketball coach at Winston-Salem State. I showed Bob Feller the picture also, and he recognized Luke Easter right away. He told me that he and Easter were once teammates. I mentioned that I was at Griffith Stadium in 1948 when the Washington Senators played against his team, the Cleveland Indians. Larry Doby came up to home plate and hit a ball to straight away centerfield, and the ball hit the public-address system on top of the wall, making the P.A. system inoperable. Bob smiled and said he remembered that game.

B. Coward's Personal Collection
James "Beanie" Howell, the 1st African-American to referee an NCAA National Championship, and Larry Hill, the 1st African-American to officiate in the instant replay booth for the Superbowl, receive an award at the Pigskin Basketball Awards Dinner

B. Coward's Personal Collection
General Elmer Brooks, Billy Coward, and Pigskin Club President Frank Bolden at Pigskin Club's Basketball Luncheon

Photo by Bob Fentriss
Family photo taken at retirement of Billy Coward from
Howard University in 1993
In front, granddaughter Brandi. L-R: daughter Donna, wife Tamara,
Billy Coward, daughter Terry, and daughter Vicki

B. Coward's Personal Collection
Coach Billy Coward poses with Quarterback Jay Walker and Wide
Receiver/Kick Returner Gary Harrell of the 1993 National Black College
Football Champion Howard University Bison, at the Pigskin Club's 56th
Annual Black Tie Awards Dinner

B. Coward's Personal Collection
From L-R: Coach John McClendon, MC Glenn Harris, Florence Griffith "Flo-Jo" Joyner, Coach Clarence "Big House" Gaines and Al Joyner after receiving plaques at the Pigskin Club's 57th Annual Awards Dinner.

B. Coward's Personal Collection
Kicking Coach Billy Coward with Rubin Ruiz (36) and Jason DeCuir (18) prior to a game at Howard University. Both kickers played on Howard's 1993 and 1996 National Black College Championship teams.

B. Coward's Personal Collection
From L-R: Pigskinner John Gamble, Howard University QB Jay Walker, WR Gary Harrell, Coach Steve Wilson, and Pigskinner Larry Frelow pose for picture after being awarded trophies at the Pigskin Club's 57th Annual Awards Dinner.

B. Coward's Personal Collection
Hall of Fame Basketball Coach John McLendon (center) and Congressman Louis Stokes (glasses), share some pleasantries at Pigskin Club's 57th Annual Awards Dinner. Hampton University's former football Coach Joe Taylor in background

All Pro Photo
Ted White, Quarterback for the Howard University Bison, leading his team to the National Black College Football Championship in 1996

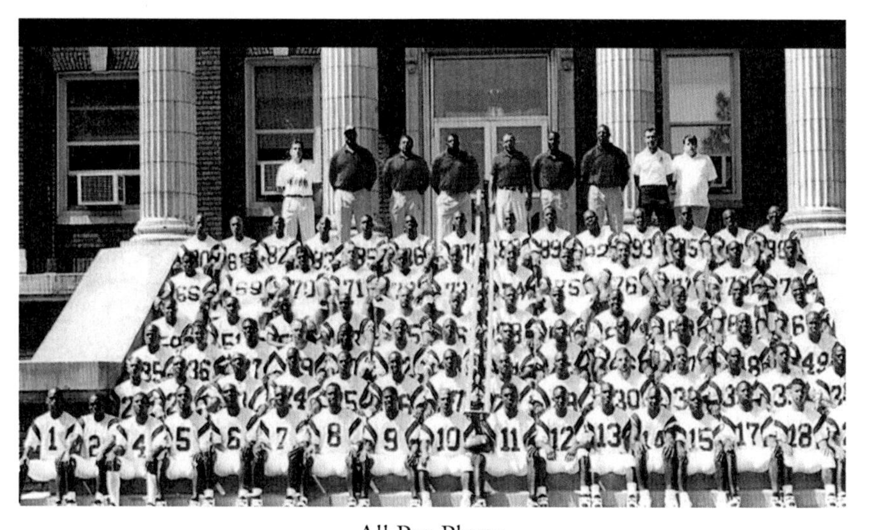

All Pro Photo
Howard University Bison 1996 National Black College Football Champions

B. Coward's Personal Collection
Howard University Football Coach Steve Wilson and QB Ted White after receiving awards at Pigskin Annual Awards Dinner for winning the 1996 Black College Football Championship

All Pro Photograph

Jermaine Holliway and Ron Williamson listen to Coach Billy Coward during Howard's victory against North Carolina A&T, January 2000.

B. Coward's Personal Collection

Billy Coward, Johnny Grier, Bob Headen, and Dr. Allen Chinn at halftime of DCPS City Championship game November 23, 2000

B. Coward's Personal Collection
Billy Coward poses with a plaque received after being inducted into the DCPS Retired Coaches Hall of Fame.

B. Coward's Personal Collection
Billy Coward receives Pigskin Service Award from Pigskin Club President Lucille Hester.

B. Coward's Personal Collection
Billy Coward with Adrian Dantley at his reception prior to Adrian's jersey retirement ceremony with the Utah Jazz, April 11, 2007

B. Coward's Personal Collection
Hall of Famer James Worthy (UNC and Los Angeles Lakers) and Billy Coward during 2008 Hall of Fame weekend

B. Coward's Personal Collection
The Pigskin Club's William G. "Billy" Coward Award presented to the National Black College Football Champions annually

B. Coward's Personal Collection
Earl Lloyd, the first African-American to play in the NBA, and Billy Coward at the Basketball Hall of Fame in 2008

B. Coward's Personal Collection
Baseball Hall of Famer Monte Irvin (New York Giants) and Billy Coward at a reception at Washington Nationals Stadium President's Club, November 7, 2008

B. Coward's Personal Collection
Baseball Hall of Famer Bob Feller (Cleveland Indians) and Billy Coward at a reception at Washington Nationals Stadium President's Club on November 7, 2008, Bob's 90th birthday

Courtesy of Frank Ceresi & Washington Nationals
A collage of pictures at Nationals Stadium including Jackie Robinson and Branch Rickey (top center), Don Zimmer and Ted Williams (top right), and President Kennedy throwing out first ball

Courtesy of Frank Ceresi & Washington Nationals
Billy Coward with his son-in-law Eric Rosen at Nationals Stadium in front of a collage of pictures including a picture of Luke Easter, Wilmer Fields, and Billy Coward (38) as batboy for the Homestead Grays

Chapter 12

DURING THE SPRING of 1985, I happened to run into Colonel Posey in the Blackburn Student Union Building on the campus of Howard University, my place of employment at the time. Colonel Posey, the former principal of Phelps High School in Washington, was the president of the Pigskin Club, which was having one of its regular meetings in the building on that particular day. We had known each other from the time when I was coaching at Bell Vocational and he was principal at Phelps. We stopped to chat, and he invited me to join the Pigskin Club during our conversation. He gave me a brief synopsis of the club and its mission. He thought I would be interested in what the club was all about because I was a former athlete and coach. He suggested that I should not have a problem in becoming a member and mentioned the particulars I would need to follow to seek membership in the club. I said I was interested and would take his advice. I subsequently completed all of the necessary steps toward membership and was voted in.

The Pigskin Club was founded by Dr. Charles B. Fisher, a former star football player at Howard from 1917 to 1920. As an athlete himself, he recognized the benefits derived from his participation in athletics, and as a physician, the occasional physical problems incidental to one's participation in the sports. Dr. Fisher conceived the idea of forming an organization of men who had participated in sports and were enthusiastic about establishing a forum through which ideas of like-minded individuals could be discussed and implemented. The first meeting of the club was held on Tuesday, July 25, 1938. In a note announcing a larger meeting a few days later, he wrote:

Dear Friend of Football,

On Saturday night, July 30, 1938, at nine o'clock, I am asking those whom I believe are interested in the formation of the Pigskin Club to meet at my home. To become a member requires no fee. The purpose and eligibility are stated on the enclosed card.

May I have the pleasure of seeing you?

Sincerely Yours,
Charles B. Fisher, MD
"Organizer"

As a result of this meeting, the Pigskin Club saw its beginning. According to information printed in all of its recent anniversary awards programs, it has been chronicled that "Since the first meeting, the Pigskin Club has become one of the leading and influential sports organizations in the nation. Under the leadership of Dr. Fisher, the club became a rallying point for college lettermen, coaches, and citizens interested in clean sports and fair play." The Pigskin Club's motto is "Democracy in Sports." The Pigskin Club of Washington is one of the oldest sports clubs in the country. Over the years, the membership has been made up of individuals from a very diverse group of professions. Initially, the Pigskin Club was an all-male African-American organization. The club's initial focus was specifically on sports, and football in particular; however, the club is concerned about other aspects of society, such as civil rights issues, law, medicine, diplomacy, and business. Individuals have been recognized and honored for their outstanding achievements in several of these categories. Since the inauguration of the Pigskin Club and Dr. Fisher's presidency, the following individuals have succeeded him in that position: John T. Rhines, 1944; James G. Tyson, 1945-1950; Isaac N.T. Cupid, 1951-1953; Lawrence A. Oxley, 1954-1973; Carl D. Coleman, 1973-1975; John W. Posey, 1975-1989; Edward J. Queen, 1989; Frank P. Bolden, 1990-1996; Brig Owens, 1996-2002; Brian Thomas, 2003; William Chesley, 2004-2007; and in 2008, Lucille Hester became the first female president and has been for the past four years.

Although the Pigskin Club was an all-male African-American organization when it was initially formed, in later years the membership became integrated by race and gender. In 2001 Lucille Hester, the project director of the NCAA youth sports program, became the first female member of the club. She was followed by Vinna I. Freeman, the first African-American female to become the supervising director of health and physical education, athletics, and driver education in the DC Public Schools.

For many years, the Pigskin Club has been hosting its annual black-tie awards dinner at the Capital Hilton Hotel, located about two blocks north of the White House. Throughout the years, a variety of awards have been given to participants in football and several other categories. Plaques in the shape of footballs were given to the Pigskin Club's All Metropolitan High School Football Team honorees. The individuals receiving the plaques comprised the All-Defensive Team, the All-Offensive Team, and the punter, kicker, and kick-return specialists. Special recognition and a trophy were awarded to the All-Metropolitan Defensive Player of the Year, the All-Metropolitan Offensive Player of the Year, and the Outstanding Scholar-Athlete of the Year. A trophy is also awarded to the All-Metropolitan High School Coach of the Year.

Several of the players selected to the Pigskin All Metropolitan High School Football Team have gone on to have successful college careers and some have gone on to play in the NFL.

Past Honorees Selected to the Pigskin All-Metropolitan High School Football Team Who Have Played in the National Football League

Name	Position	High School Attended
Lamont Jordan	Running Back	Suitland
Jared Gaither	Defensive Lineman	Eleanor Roosevelt
Byron Leftwich	Quarterback	H.D. Woodson
Jonathan Ogden	Offensive Lineman	St. Albans
Cato June	Defensive Back	Anacostia
Evan Royster	Offensive Back	Westfield
Arrelious Benn	Wide Receiver	Dunbar
Marvin Austin	Defensive Lineman	Ballou
Vernon Davis	Tight End	Dunbar
Vontae Davis	Defensive Back	Dunbar
Joshua Cribbs	Wide Receiver/Kick Returner	Dunbar
Aloysius Chesley	Linebacker	Eastern

Various Pigskin Club awards named in honor of Pigskin legends have been granted to high school coaches, scholar athletes, outstanding high school players, NCAA coaches of the year, NCAA players of the year, and others throughout the years.

Recipients of Awards Named for Pigskin Club Legends

Award Named for Pigskin Club Legend	Intended Recipient
The Edward Henderson Award	High School Coach of the Year
The Rodney P. Savoy Award	Outstanding High School Scholar Athlete
The Leonard Guy Ford, Jr. Award	Outstanding Defensive High School Player of the Year
The Charles Richard Drew Award	NCAA Division I Coach of the Year
The John L. Young Award	NCAA Division I Offensive Player of the Year
The Lawrence Agustus Oxley Award	NCAA Division I Defensive Player of the Year
The W. Henry "Stud" Green Award	CIAA Coach of the Year
The James Guy "Pete" Tyson Award	CIAA Player of the Year
The Talmadge L. "Marse" Hill Award	MEAC Coach of the Year
The Cato W. Adams Award	MEAC Player of the Year
The Charles R. Fisher Award	SIAC Coach of the Year
The Oliver M. Thompson Award	SIAC Player of the Year
The Tillman Sease Award	SWAC Coach of the Year
The Paul Duffy Award	SWAC Player of the Year
The John W. Posey Award	Outstanding Professional Athlete of the Year
The Frank P. Bolden Trophy	All-Metropolitan College Player of the Year
The Sylvester "Sal" Hall Trophy	NCAA Quarterback of the Year

Other awards traditionally given out not necessarily related to one's involvement in football are the Pigskin Club Special Recognition Award, the Pigskin Club Award of Excellence, the Pigskin Club Community Service Award, the Pigskin Club Award of Honor, and the Youth Sports and Life Skills Program Award, which recognizes a local student.

Throughout the years, the club has recognized and honored many of the National Collegiate Athletic Association's outstanding football coaches and athletic directors. Some of these individuals were Earl C. Banks, Morgan State; Bobby Bowden, Florida State; Clarence Gaines, Winston-Salem State; Jake Gaither, Florida A&M; Lou Holtz, Notre Dame; Willie Jeffries, South Carolina State; Vernon McCain, Maryland State; Joseph P. Paterno, Penn State; Bert Piggot, North Carolina A&T; Pete Richardson, Southern; Edward Robinson, Grambling State; Joe Taylor, Hampton; Steve Wilson, Howard; and Jim Tressel, Ohio State.

The club has also honored a number of the National Collegiate Athletic Association All-American football players in the NCAA.

NCAA All-American Football Players Honored by the Pigskin Club

Name of Player	NCAA College Attended
Robert Butkus	Illinois
Cornell Davis	Winston-Salem State
Tony Dorsett	Pittsburgh
Larry Fitzgerald	Pittsburgh
Cornelius Green	Ohio State
Gary "Flea" Harrell	Howard
James Earl Harvey	North Carolina Central
Bo Jackson	Auburn
Dan Marino	Pittsburgh
Steve McNair	Alcorn State
Leo Miles	Virginia State
Bobby Mitchell	Illinois
Lennie Moore	Penn State
Harvey Reed	Howard
John Sample	Maryland State
Leroy Selmon	Oklahoma
Roger Staubach	US Naval Academy
Jay Walker	Howard
Ted White	Howard
Claude "Buddy" Young	Illinois

Other honorees who received awards under a variety of categories through the years were:

- Ken Beatrice, WMAL Sports Call
- Mike Tyson, Boxing Heavyweight Champion
- Thomas "The Hitman" Hearns, Boxing Champion, four titles in different divisions
- Polly Shackelton, Council Member in DC's Ward 3
- John B. McLendon, Jr., North Carolina Central University and Tennessee A&I Basketball Coach
- Vernon Jordan, former Urban League President
- Althea Gibson, Tennis
- Wilma Rudolph, Track
- Florence "Flo Jo" Griffith Joyner, Track, 1988 Olympics, 3 gold medals
- Sugar Ray Leonard, Boxing
- Clarence "Big House" Gaines, Coach & Athletic Director, Winston-Salem State University
- Eleanor Holmes Norton, US Congresswoman
- Jair Lynch, Olympic Gymnast, 2nd African-American to compete as a gymnast in the Olympics
- J.C. Hayward, CBS, WUSA Channel 9, News Anchor
- Charles Ramsey, District of Columbia Chief of Police
- Major Charles A. Moose, Montgomery Country of MD Chief of Police
- George Allen, Jr. former Senator from Virginia
- Charles Mann, Defensive End, Washington Redskins
- Jim Lachey, Tackle, Washington Redskins
- Art Monk, Wide Receiver, Washington Redskins
- Brian Mitchell, Running Back, Washington Redskins
- Ken Harvey, Line Backer, Washington Redskins
- Darrell Green, Defensive Back, Washington Redskins
- Trent Green, Quarterback, Washington Redskins
- Jon Jansen, Tackle, Washington Redskins
- Donna M. Wilkinson, Running Back, DC Divas
- Samuel H. Lacy, Sportswriter, Pigskin Club Hall of Fame Inductee
- Bobby Mitchell, Special Tribute, Redskins Player and Administrator

- Brig Owens, Living Legend, Washington Redskins and past President of the Pigskin Club

Other awards which have been presented are The Pigskin Club Special Recognition Award; the Pigskin Club Award of Excellence; the Pigskin Club Community Service Award; and the Pigskin Club Award of Honor.

I think it is worth mentioning that several members of the Pigskin Club were or are current NFL or NBA officials. In the NFL, Boris Cheek is currently a back judge; James Duke was a former umpire; Johnny Grier was a former referee; and Larry Upson was a former supervisor of officials. In the NBA, Sean Cordin and Luis Grillo were both referees. Additionally, "Bullet" Bob Hayes, the brother of Lucille Hester, the president of the club, is the only athlete in history to win an Olympic gold medal and a Super Bowl ring. Bob won two gold medals in the 1964 Olympic games in Tokyo, Japan, and he was a member of the Dallas Cowboys team when they won the Super Bowl VI Championship.

In 2006 the Pigskin Club began presenting the William G. "Billy" Coward Trophy to the National Black College Football Champions. Since then the trophy has been awarded to six HBCU institutions.

Recipients of the William G. "Billy" Coward Trophy

Institution	Year	Record
North Carolina Central University Eagles	2006	11 wins, 0 losses
Tuskegee University Golden Tigers	2007	12 wins, 0 losses
Grambling State University Tigers	2008	11 wins, 2 losses
South Carolina State University Bulldogs	2009	10 wins, 2 losses
Albany State University Golden Rams	2010	11 wins, 1 loss
Winston-Salem State University Rams	2011	13 wins, 1 loss

As the years passed, I was able to meet and interact with a number of the honorees at the club's Annual Awards Dinner. In 1993 when the club honored Coach John McLendon and Coach Clarence "Bighouse" Gaines, I remembered when each of them served as clinicians at a basketball clinic sponsored by Federal City College when I was the basketball coach at that institution. Also being honored was Florence Griffith Joyner. She was accompanied by her husband and coach, Al Joyner. I remember after "Flo Jo" won three gold medals in the 1988 Olympics, he stated in an interview that he had her doing something while she was running that enabled her to be so successful, but he never revealed publicly what that "something" was. So, I asked him when we had an opportunity to converse at the awards dinner, what that something was. He said, "Relaxing." I thought that he had her doing something really special. When he told me that the secret to her success was to relax as she ran, I told him my college coach and instructor Dr. Leroy T. Walker had told me the same thing when I was in college and I too found it to be very effective.

The 1993 Pigskin Awards Dinner was also a special affair for me personally. That year the Howard University football team had won the National Black College Football Championship. Because I was the kicking coach on that team as well as a member of the club it was very satisfying to me to see other individuals who were a part of the team receive recognition and honor by the Pigskin Club for their accomplishments. Jay "Sky" Walker, the team's quarterback, was honored as the NCAA and MEAC Quarterback of the Year. Gary "The Flea" Harrell was honored as the Metropolitan Area Collegiate Offensive Player of the Year, and Steve Wilson, the team's coach, was selected as the NCAA Coach of the Year.

During one of our annual Pigskin Awards Dinner affairs, I saw Glenn Harris, the MC that night, in the company of Mark Moseley, the Redskins' place kicker. Mark was unique because he kicked off, kicked extra points, and also kicked field goals using the old straight-ahead method of kicking from the toe of his shoe. In this day and age, kickers are using the soccer-style method of kicking, and the ball is kicked with the instep rather than the toe. Mark had won the MVP award in the NFL in 1982 as a kicker – the only place kicker to receive this award in the history of the NFL. Glenn saw me and asked if I had met Mark before. I told him that I had not. I introduced myself and my son-in-law, Eric Rosen, who was with me. I told him that I was the kicking coach at Howard University and indicated I would like to know if he had any suggestions that might help the kickers whom I coached. Mark said, "It seems that they are doing very well. I read about them, in the paper." *The Washington Post* had run an article with a picture of the kickers, Ruben Ruiz and Jason DeCuir, and me. In that article the kickers were given credit for being a reliable part of the success that Howard was having during that particular football season. Mark continued, "Just tell the kickers to kick the football straight." I looked at him and said, "Pardon?" He repeated, "Just tell them to kick the football straight." Eric looked at me, and we both smiled. I said to Mark, "I have been telling them to do that regularly, but I was hoping that you may have known about some unique techniques or exercises that might further enhance their ability to kick the football." Ruben and Jason continued to kick the ball straight and continued to be successful in doing so.

In 1996 as I continued to work with the Howard Bison as the kicking coach, they won the National Black College Championship for the second time in four years. This time the team quarterback was Ted "Sweet Flight" White, who was recognized as the Pigskin Club's MEAC Player of the Year as well as the Washington Metropolitan Area Collegiate Offensive Player of the Year. Steve was again selected as the MEAC Coach of the Year.

At the Pigskin Club's 2011 Awards Dinner, Natalie Randolph, the head football coach at Calvin Coolidge High School and the first female high school football coach in the DC Public Schools, won the Edwin B. Henderson Award as the High School Coach of the Year.

Chapter 13

WE HAVE OFTEN heard that personal experiences mold one's character and shape one's future in so many ways. As I reflect on my many experiences in the world of sports, I believe there is some truth to this opinion. For more than seventy years, I have been involved in sports at one level or another – most of them team sports. When I was young, I played football, basketball, and baseball in the streets or alleys with other kids in the neighborhood. There were no referees or adults to monitor us as we played, and oftentimes these moments of fun would turn into acts of aggression when one or more individuals did not play by the rules. Moments such as this required us to resolve our differences in a manner amenable to the group. We either decided to 1) enforce existing rules, if there were any or 2) establish new rules. Thus, we learned the art of diplomacy which carried over into other experiences later in life. Of course, if there was no compromise, the individual who owned the ball simply took his ball and went home, leaving the rest of us to look for something else to do with our time. Either scenario may also have taught us how to be flexible in difficult situations. As the saying goes, "If you are not flexible in a hurricane, you become uprooted."

As a high-school athlete, I was very fortunate to receive some recognition as a result of my performance on the football field and, consequently, was fortunate enough to have been offered a scholarship to play football on the college level. Several of my high-school and college friends who were accomplished athletes in their own rights and I have established a social and professional network of individuals who have been supportive of each other in a number of different ways over the years.

As a participant and as a coach, I was on both ends of the spectrum and experienced the emotional highs and lows of a game –the thrill of winning as well as the agonizing lows of defeat. But I learned that by continuing to persevere despite all odds, we at least had an opportunity to remain competitive. This too is a lesson that has carried me through life.

After more than seventy years of active involvement in sports as a participant or coach, I now find my involvement pretty much limited to that of spectator. Nonetheless, as a sports-minded individual, I continue to stress the importance of sports and physical exercise as a part of a healthy lifestyle. As with my daughters when they were small, I have tried to encourage my grandchildren to get involved in sports and now attend their activities as often as possible. When my granddaughter, Brandi, was about six, she was introduced to basketball at a local recreation center. She developed such a passion for the sport that she continued to play in the AAU league, then in high school with the Lady Falcons at Good Counsel Catholic High School. During the 2000-2001 basketball season at Good Counsel, she won a trophy for being the team's leading scorer and the Most Valuable Player on the team; and the following year she again earned recognition as the team's leading scorer. She continued to pursue her passion for basketball on the college level at West Virginia Wesleyan, where she was a starting player for the majority of her four years there. My wife and I supported her during those years by attending as many of her games as we possibly could. Today she is coaching a junior high school team, and we continue to support her and her team as spectators. Our grandson, Justin, has been introduced to many sports – tennis, soccer, basketball, lacrosse, and swimming – and we have watched many of his activities also, but he did not find one in which he had a real interest until he was introduced to skateboarding a few years ago. Now that seems to be a true passion of his.

Although I no longer play sports, I still swim and work out in the fitness center at the Aspen Hill Club, occasionally take in a live football or basketball game, and, of course, watch as much basketball, football, baseball, track, tennis, and swimming on TV as I can fit into an otherwise fairly active life as a retiree. What a tremendous ride it has been: my exposure to sports.

Acknowledgements

To the many individuals – friends and family – who have encouraged me over the years to put my words to print, to those who have assisted me in recalling names, dates, and events that were an important part of this book, and to others who have assisted me in so many different ways since I started this project, I extend my sincere thanks.

I especially thank my wife, Tamara, for tirelessly assisting me in the completion of the manuscript and for sharing with me her own experiences as a writer and published author, which helped to facilitate the process for me.

I thank my granddaughter, Brandi N. Wynn, for undertaking the creation of the graphic design for the book and for her tireless efforts to work with me as we completed the tasks of copying, arranging, and completing the captions for the pictures used in this book, which provide a pictorial story to support the narrative.

References

Adrian Dantley, Jersey Retirement Program, April 11, 2007, Utah Jazz vs. Denver Nuggets.

Basketball Hall of Fame Class of 2008 Program.

Driscoll, Laura, Negro Leagues: All-Black Baseball; New York: Grosset & Dunlap Publisher, 2002.

History of American Negro – North Carolina Edition, Vol. IV, A.B. Caldwell Publishing Co., Copyright 1921.

Howard Bison Football Media Guide, 1999.

Howard University's Howard Magazine Alumni News, October 1966; An Alumnus Looks Back After 75 Years, Football is Greatest Memory.

Inventor Charles Richard Drew, Biography, www.ideafinder.com/history/inventors/drew.htm.

Ninth Capital Classic Souvenir Program.

North Carolina Central University at a Glance, www.edu/aboutnccu/history.cfm.

The Pigskin Club's 50th Anniversary Annual Awards Program.

The Pigskin Club's 56th Annual Awards Dinner Program.

The Pigskin Club's 59th Annual Awards Dinner Program.

The Pigskin Club's 60th Annual Awards Dinner Program.

2006 CIAA Basketball Tournament Program.

2009 MEAC Basketball Tournament Program.

Index